# Dorchester in 1630, 1776, and 1855.

---

AN

# ORATION

## DELIVERED ON THE FOURTH OF JULY, 1855,

BY

EDWARD EVERETT.

---

ALSO

## AN ACCOUNT OF THE PROCEEDINGS

IN DORCHESTER

AT THE CELEBRATION OF THE DAY.

---

BOSTON:
PRINTED AND PUBLISHED BY DAVID CLAPP.
EBENEZER CLAPP, Jr.....184 WASHINGTON ST.
1855.

*Dorchester, July* 13, 1855.

HON. EDWARD EVERETT,—

MY DEAR SIR:

I have the honor herewith to transmit a Resolution of the Executive Committee for the late celebration in Dorchester, which passed that body with perfect unanimity.

Permit me also to express the sense of gratitude which the Committee, in common with their fellow citizens, feel for the most acceptable service performed by you on that occasion, and to hope that it may suit your convenience to place early in our hands, a copy of your very learned and eloquent Oration for publication.

With profound respect, your obd't servant,

MARSHALL P. WILDER.

—

*Dorchester, July* 9, 1855.

At a meeting of the Executive Committee for the Celebration of the Settlement of Dorchester and the Seventy-ninth Anniversary of the Independence of the United States, it was—

*Resolved*, That the thanks of the Committee be tendered to the Hon. Edward Everett for his eloquent, instructive, and truly patriotic Address delivered upon that occasion, and that a copy of it be requested for publication.

MARSHALL P. WILDER,
E. P. TILESTON,
DANIEL DENNY,
WILLIAM D. SWAN,
NAHUM CAPEN,
ENOCH TRAIN,
OLIVER HALL,
LEWIS PIERCE,
NATHAN CARRUTH,
E. J. BISPHAM,
JNO. H. ROBINSON,
CHARLES HUNT,
EDWARD KING.

---

*Boston,* 15 *July,* 1855.

MY DEAR SIR,—

I have received your letter of the 13th, with the resolution of the Executive Committee for the late Celebration in Dorchester, requesting a copy of my Oration delivered on the 4th instant.

I am much indebted to the Committee for their favorable estimate of my Address, and cheerfully place it at their disposal.

Be pleased to accept my acknowledgments for the kind terms with which you have conveyed the request of the Committee, and believe me, dear Sir, with great regard,

Very truly yours,

EDWARD EVERETT.

Hon. MARSHALL P. WILDER.

# DEDICATION.

---

To the Inhabitants of both Sexes of my Native Town this Oration is, with warm Gratitude for the sympathizing Attention with which it was heard by them,

Respectfully and affectionately

Dedicated, by

EDWARD EVERETT.

# INTRODUCTORY NOTE.

The following Oration is printed from the manuscript as originally prepared (of which about a third part was omitted in speaking in consequence of its length), with the addition as far as recollected of what suggested itself in the delivery.

Besides the original authorities cited in their appropriate places, I would make a general acknowledgment of my obligations to the "Chronological and Topographical Account of Dorchester," by Rev. Dr. Harris, in the ninth volume of the first series of the Collections of the Massachusetts Historical Society, and to the three numbers of the "History of Dorchester," now in course of publication by a committee of the Antiquarian and Historical Society of that town. Other interesting materials, of which my limits did not permit me to make much use, were placed in my hands by Dr. T. W. Harris, partly from the manuscripts of his venerable father; by Mr. Nahum Capen on the connection of Roger Sherman with Dorchester; by Mr. Ebenezer Clapp, jr. on the subject of the Midway Church; and by Mr. Daniel Denny, from a memorandum of the late Mr. J. Smith Boies, on the occupation of Dorchester Heights. If those acquainted with the history of our ancient town should be disappointed at finding some matters of interest wholly passed over, and others lightly treated, they will be pleased to reflect upon the difficulty of doing justice to all parts of a subject so comprehensive, within the limits of a popular address.

In the narrative of the occupation of Dorchester Heights, I have followed the safe guidance of the "History of the Siege of Boston," by Mr. R. Frothingham, jr.

It may be thought ungracious, at the present day, to dwell with emphasis on the oppressive measures of the Colonial Government, which caused the American Revolution, and on the military incidents of the contest. I believe, however, that no greater service could be rendered to humanity than to present the essential abuses and inevitable results of colonial rule in such a light to the Governments of Western Europe, and especially to the English Government as that most concerned, as will lead to the systematic adoption of the course suggested on page 77 of this discourse;—that is, the amicable concession to colonies, mature for self-government, of that independence which will otherwise be extorted by mutually exhausting wars.

Among the novel lessons of higher politics taught in our constitutional history, as yet but little reflected on at home, and well worth the profound study of statesmen in the constitutional governments of Europe, is the peaceful separation from parent States of territories as large as many a European kingdom; an event of which five or six instances have occurred since the formation of the Federal Union, under whose auspices these separations have taken place.

*Boston, July*, 1855.

# ORATION.

Among the numerous calls to address public meetings with which I have been honored during my life, I have never received one with greater pleasure, than that which brings me before you this day. Drawn up with unusual precision and care by a skilful pen, subscribed by more than one hundred and fifty of your leading citizens, and placed in my hands by a most respected committee of their number, it apprizes me that "the citizens of Dorchester, without distinction of party, actuated by motives of public good, and believing in the salutary teaching of national events, when contemplated with an inquiring spirit and an enlightened judgment, are desirous of celebrating the 4th of July, 1854, in a manner that shall prove creditable to that ancient town, instructive to the young, renovating to the aged, and morally profitable to the nation," and it invites me, as a native citizen of the town, to join you in carrying this purpose into effect.

You are well acquainted, Fellow-citizens, with the circumstances that prevented my appearing before you last year, in pursuance of this invitation. I might still, without impropriety, offer you a sufficient excuse, in the state of my health, for shrinking from the effort of addressing an audience like this; and I feel deeply my inability, under any circumstances, to fulfil the conditions of your invitation as I have just repeated them. But I confess I have not been able to forego this first opportunity, the last, also, no doubt, I shall ever enjoy, of publicly addressing the citizens of Dorchester; — the place of my birth, of my early education, and of all the kindly associations of my childhood. I have felt an irresistible attraction to the spot. I behold around me the originals of the earliest impressions upon my mind, which neither time nor the cares of a crowded life have effaced. Some fifty-six or seven years have passed since, as a school-boy, I climbed,—summer and winter,—what then seemed to me the steep acclivity of Meeting-house hill. The old School-house (it was then the new School-house, but I recollect that which preceded it) has disappeared. The ancient Church in which I was baptized, is no longer standing. The venerable pastor,* whose affectionate smile still lives in the memory of so many who listen to me, has ceased from his labors. The entire generation to whom I looked up as to aged or even grown men, are departed; but the images of all that has passed away have been cast and abide, with more than photographic truth, upon the inmost chambers of my memory. Some of us, my friends, companions of school-boy days, remain to cherish the thought of the past, to meditate on the lapse of years and the

* Rev. Dr Harris.

events they have brought forth, and to rejoice in the growth and improvement of our native town. We have pursued different paths in life; Providence has sent us into various fields of duty and usefulness, of action and suffering: but I am sure there is not one of us who has wandered or who has remained, that does not still feel a dutiful interest in the place of his birth; and who does not experience something more than usual sensibility on an occasion like this.

In those things, which in a rapidly improving community are subject to change, there are few places, within my knowledge, which within fifty years have undergone greater changes than Dorchester. The population in 1800 was 2347; in 1850 it was a little short of 8000. What was then called "the Neck," the most secluded portion of the old town, although the part which led to its being first pitched upon as a place of settlement, was in 1804 annexed to Boston; and being united with the city by two bridges, has long since exchanged the retirement of a village for the life and movement of the metropolis. The pick-axe is making sad ravages upon one of the venerable heights of Dorchester; the entrenchments of the other, no longer masking the deadly enginery of war, are filled with the refreshing waters of Cochituate lake. New roads have been opened in every part of our ancient town, and two railways traverse it from north to south. The ancient houses built before the revolution have not all disappeared, but they are almost lost in the multitude of modern dwellings. A half century ago there was but one church in the town, that which stood on yonder hill, and the school-house which then stood by its side was, till 1802, the only one dignified by the name of a Town School. You have now ten churches and seven school-houses of the first class;—and all the establishments of an eminently prosperous town, situated in the vicinity of a great commercial metropolis, have multiplied in equal proportion.

But all is not changed. The great natural features of the scene, and no where are they more attractive, are of course unaltered:—the same fine sweep of the shore with its projecting headlands,—the same extensive plain at the North part of the town,—the same gentle undulations and gradual ascent to the South,—the same beautiful elevations. I caught a few days ago, from the top of Jones's hill, the same noble prospect (and I know not a finer on the coast of Massachusetts), which used to attract my boyish gaze more than fifty years ago. Old hill, as we called it then (it has lost that venerable name in the progress of refinement, though it has become half a century older), notwithstanding the tasteful villas which adorn its base, exhibits substantially the same native grouping of cedars and the same magnificent rocks, and commands the same fine view of the harbor, which it did before a single house was built within its precincts. Venerable trees that seemed big to me in my boyhood,—I have been looking at some of them this morning,—seem but little bigger now, though I trace the storms of fifty winters on some well-recollected branches. The aged sycamores which shaded the roof, beneath which I was born, still shade it; and the ancient burial ground hard by, with which there are few of us who have not some tender associations, upon whose early graves may yet be seen the massy unhewn stones placed there by the first settlers for protection against the wolves, still attracts the antiquary with its quaint and learned inscriptions, and preserves the memory not merely of "the rude forefathers of the hamlet," but of some of the most honored names in the history of Massachusetts.

But I ought to apologize, my friends, for dwelling on topics so deeply tinged with personal recollection. The occasion on which we are met invites all our thoughts to public themes. It is two hundred and twenty-five years since the commencement of the settlement of our ancient town,—the first foothold of the pioneers of Governor Winthrop's expedition. It is the seventy-ninth anniversary of the Declaration of the Independence of the United States. Our minds naturally go back to the foundations of the ancient Commonwealth of which we are citizens, laid as they were within our limits. We dwell with pleasure and pride on the growth of our native town under the vicissitudes of colonial fortune, from its feeble beginnings to the dimensions of a large and flourishing municipality; and we meditate with just interest upon those eventful scenes at the commencement of the Revolutionary War of which our heights were the theatre, and which exerted an undoubted influence upon the Continental Congress at Philadelphia in hastening the Great Declaration.

Thus the appropriate topics of the day correspond

with the three great divisions, which make up the whole system of political philosophy. We have, first, The foundation of a State,—the measures and agencies by which, under Providence, a new people is called into the family of nations;—manifestly the most important event, humanly speaking, that can occur in the history of our race. Second, We have the institutions and events which make up the political life of a community;—the organization and action, by which the divinely appointed ordinance of civil government is administered, so as best to promote the welfare and progress of a people. Third, We have one of those great movements called Revolutions, by which a people for urgent causes introduces organic changes in the frame-work of its government, and materially renovates or wholly reconstructs the fabric of its political relations.

In reference to each of these three great branches of political science, the history of our ancient town and the occasion which calls us together furnish us with the most striking illustrations and instructive lessons. The foundation of a new State, in a quarter of the globe before unknown, is an event without a parallel in the domain of authentic history. The time and the manner in which the earliest predecessors of the present inhabitants of Europe became established there, are but imperfectly known; while the first settlement of Asia and Africa, after the original dispersion of mankind, is lost in those unfathomable depths of antiquity, which the deep sea-line of research has never sounded. It is only after comparing the authentic pages of our early history with the clouds of insipid fable that hang over the origin of Athens, and Rome, and Great Britain,—fables which neither Plutarch, nor Livy, nor Milton has been able to raise into dignity and interest,—that we perceive the real grandeur of the work of which the foundations were laid two centuries and a quarter ago on Dorchester plain.

So with respect to the second branch of political philosophy, the organization and administration of States, I am disposed to affirm that there are secrets of practical wisdom and prudence, — elements of growth and prosperity, — in our municipal system, which deserve to be thoughtfully explored. Our towns of course are but units in the great sum which makes up the State. They possess none of the higher powers of government. Not by their hands is wielded the mace of legislation, or the scales of justice, the purse or the sword of the Commonwealth. But whenever the prosperity of New England and the younger States modelled on its type is traced to its ultimate causes, it will be found to a good degree in this municipal system. In the pages of these ancient volumes, — these old town records which have in few cases been better preserved than in Dorchester,—there will be found lessons of experience, of blessed common sense shaping itself to the exigency of uncommon times, of patient submission to present evils in the hope of a brighter day, of fortitude and courage in an humble sphere, of provident care for the rising generation and posterity, of unwearied diligence for the promotion of religion, morals, and education, which in their joint effect have done much toward giving us this goodly heritage.

Lastly, of those great movements by which organic changes are wrought in established governments and a new order in the political world brought in, it must be admitted that the event which we commemorate to-day, in the character of the parties,—an infant confederacy of republics just starting out of a state of colonial pupilage on the one hand, and one of the oldest monarchies in Europe on the other; the long and silent preparation and the gradual approach; the soundness of the principles which impelled the movement, acknowledged as it was by the most illustrious statesmen of the mother country; the purity and pristine simplicity of manners that characterized the revolutionary leaders; the almost total absence of those violent and sanguinary incidents that usually mark the progress of civil war; and the gradual development, out of the chaos of the struggle, of well-balanced systems of republican government and federal union;—in all these respects, it must be allowed, that there is a solitary dignity and elevation in our American Revolution. They make it perhaps the only instance in history of the severance of a mighty empire, equally to the advantage of the new state and the parent country; the single case of a rising republic not built upon the calamitous ruins of earlier organizations.

You will readily perceive, my friends, that the thorough treatment of this subject in all its parts would occupy much more time than can be reasonably devoted to a public address; and that in attempting to embrace them all in the remarks I venture to offer you, I must wholly omit some important topics and pass lightly over others.

It is impossible fully to comprehend the importance of the work which was accomplished in the colonization of America, without regarding it as a part of the great plan of Providence, in disposing the time and circumstances of the discovery of our continent;—hidden as it was till the end of the fifteenth century from the rest of the world. This thought was brought so forcibly to my mind a few years since by a circumstance personal to myself, that I think you will pardon me for alluding to it, though in itself of a trifling domestic character. In the year 1841, I occupied with my family the Villa Careggi, near Florence, once, as its name imports (*Casa regia*), a princely residence, belonging to the Grand Duke of Tuscany, but of late years private property, and occasionally leased to travellers.* Half fortress, half palace, it was built by Cosmo de' Medici in 1444, nine years before the capture of Constantinople by the Ottomans in 1453. By that appalling event, a barbarous race (which had issued from the depths of Asia some centuries before, and had engrafted the Mahometan imposture on the primitive stock of Tartarian paganism) had stormed the last stronghold of

* Roscoe's Lorenzo de' Medici, p. 292. This most interesting Villa remained a part of the Grand ducal domain till 1788, when with other estates it was sold by the Grand Duke Leopold from motives of economy. It has lately passed into the possession of Mr. Sloane, an English gentleman of taste and fortune, by whom the grounds and approaches have been greatly improved, and the whole establishment restored to something like its original magnificence.

the ancient civilization, the metropolis of the Greek empire, and established the religion of the Koran at the heart of the old world. The relations of the Turks to the rest of Europe are so entirely changed, that it is now scarcely possible to conceive the terror caused by this event. Had nothing occurred to renovate and strengthen the civilization of the west, it is not easy to imagine what might have been at this day the condition of Christendom. Even as it was, the Sultan was for two centuries forward the strongest military power in the world; the scourge and the terror of the Mediterranean, and the master of some of the finest provinces of Eastern Europe.

But germs of revival sprung up from the ruins of the old civilization. A host of learned and ingenious men, Christian scholars, fled from the edge of the Turkish scimetar and took refuge in Italy. They were received with hospitality there, and especially by the merchant princes of Florence. The Platonic Academy was established in the arcades of the Villa Careggi. A great intellectual restoration took place in Italy, and spread rapidly to the west of Europe, where precisely at the same time the Art of Printing (after slowly struggling through successive stages in the cities of the Netherlands and the Rhine) burst upon the world in a state approaching perfection and not surpassed at the present day. The stores of learning and thought accumulated by the mind of antiquity were thrown open to the world. The modern bar and Senate were not yet created, and philosophy stammered in the jargon of the schools; but Cicero, and Demosthenes, and Plato, stepped forth from the dusty alcoves of monkish libraries, and again spoke to living, acting men. The pulpit of the golden-lipped St. Chrysostom was hushed, but Moses and the prophets, the Evangelists and the Apostles rose, if I may venture to say so, as from the dead. The glorious invention was inaugurated in a manner worthy of itself. Two years only after the Koran began to be read at Constantinople (just four centuries ago this year), the Bible went forth on the wings of the press to the four quarters of the world.* Mahomet the second had struck down the last Christian emperor; but Fust, and Schœffer, and Guttenberg, the Strasburg printers, aimed a deadlier blow at Mahomet the first, his code of barbarism, and all the hosts of political and spiritual darkness throughout the world. The walls of Byzantium, spouting torrents of unquenchable flame, had crumbled; but the mind of the world rallied to the new combat under the living artillery of the press, and came off victorious. A conflict more important to humanity, was never waged on earth. And from that day to this, the civilized world of Europe and America is indebted for that superiority which no second night of ignorance can darken, no new incursion of van-

---

* My much valued friend, Mr. George Livermore of Cambridge, possesses a leaf on vellum, from an imperfect copy of the Mazarin Bible, the first book ever printed, and which, though without date, is known to have been completed in 1455, and a copy of the New Testament from the Bible of 1462, the first Bible printed with a date. "A metrical exhortation," says Mr. Hallam, "in the German language *to take arms against the Turks,* dated in 1454, has been retrieved in the present century. If this date unequivocally refers to the time of printing, which does not seem a necessary consequence, it is the earliest loose sheet that is known to be extant."—Literature of Europe, Part I., Chap. III., Sec. 23.

dalism can overthrow, to an enlightened, conscientious, independent press.

But Providence had other instrumentalities in store; higher counsels. A broader field of development was to be opened to renovated humanity. The East of Europe and the West of Asia, by nature and position the fairest region of the old world, was relapsing into barbarism, but the hour had arrived to "redress the balance of empire and call into existence a new world in the West." At the close of the century which witnessed these extraordinary events, a Genoese mariner, declined from the meridian of life, in pursuit of a vision which he had cherished through years of enthusiasm and disappointment, seeking a sovereign truth through the paths of sagacious but erroneous theory, launched forth, the living compass his pilot and the constellated heavens his only chart, to find a western passage to India, and discovered a new world. A Florentine navigator, following in his track, completed his discoveries, projected them on the map, and (oh, vanity of human renown), in spite of geography and history, in spite of orators and poets, in spite of the indignant reclamations of all succeeding ages, forever stamped upon the new found continent the name of a man who did *not* first discover it, almost before the ashes were cold of the man who did!

Thus, then, we have two of the elementary conditions of the political, moral, and religious restoration about to be effected in the order of Providence, at a moment when an overshadowing cloud of Mahometan barbarism had shot rapidly toward the zenith, and seemed about to settle down on the Christian world. We have a general excitement in the Western mind, produced by the revival of the ancient learning, the art of printing, and other conspiring causes which I have not time to enumerate, and we have the boundless spaces of a new hemisphere, opened to the commerce, the adventure, and the ambition, in a word, to the quickened thought and reviving life of the old world.

But something further is wanting: a third condition is required, which should draw the two already existing into efficient coöperation; and that was the impulse and the motive, the moral machinery, the social inducement, the political necessity, which should bring the reviving intelligence of the age into fruitful action upon this vast new theatre, for the joint benefit of America and Europe, and the solid foundation of a higher civilization than the world had yet seen.

In the Villa Careggi, which I have just named, Lorenzo de' Medici, the merchant dictator of Florence, died, and his son Giovanni was born; created, through the influence of his fond father, an Abbot at the age of seven years, a Cardinal at thirteen, and raised to the papal throne at the age of thirty-eight, as Pope Leo X.* This aspiring, liberal and mu-

* The Villa Careggi is still supplied with water from a very deep well in the court yard, into which, according to a still existing but unfounded tradition, the servants of Lorenzo threw his physician for having, as they supposed, poisoned their master.—Roscoe follows the writers who represent Leo the tenth as born in Florence; but other writers and the local traditions make Careggi his birth-place. An extraordinary list of his early preferments is given by Roscoe, Leo X., Vol. I., p. 12.

nificent Pontiff, who, regarded as a secular prince, was, with all his faults, the most enlightened sovereign of his age, cradled in all the luxuries of worldly power, nursed at the bosom of the arts, raised to the throne of the then undivided church in early manhood, devoted his short but brilliant reign to two main objects, viz.:—the expulsion of the Turks from Europe, and the completion of the Church of St. Peter's at Rome, the most splendid and costly structure of human hands, and designed by him to be the great Metropolitan Temple of Universal Christendom. Who can blame him, with the genius and taste of Michael Angelo and Raphael at his command, for the generous ambition? To defray the enormous expenditure incurred by these and other measures of magnificence and policy, Leo resorted to the famous sale of indulgences throughout the Christian world. The mind of Western and Northern Europe had been warming and kindling for a century and a half toward the reformation; the sale of indulgences was the torch in the hands of Luther which lighted the flame.

Some of the German princes put themselves at the head of this great popular revolution, which was in reality the movement of the age toward civil and religious liberty; but Henry VIII. of England was one of its earliest opponents. I have held in my hand, in the library of the Vatican, the identical copy of his book against Luther, sent by Henry to Pope Leo the Tenth, which acquired for him and all his successors the cheaply earned title of "Defender of the Faith." A few years passed by; new light, kindled at no spiritual altar, shone into his mind; Catherine of Arragon was repudiated; Anne Boleyn was married, and the supremacy of the Pope abjured by Henry VIII.

This certainly was not the Reformation, but, in the hands of that Providence, which sometimes shapes base means to worthy ends, it was a step toward it. After the decease of the remorseless and sensual monarch, the conscience of England took up the work which his licentiousness and ambition began. The new opinions gained credit and extension rapidly, but with fearful dependence on the vicissitudes of the State. The service and ritual of the Church of England, substantially as they exist at this day, were established under Edward VI.; but his sister Mary, married to Philip II., the man who caused his own son to be assassinated for the good of his soul,* restored the old faith and kindled the fires of Smithfield.

With the accession of Elizabeth, the Church of England was cautiously restored, and Protestantism again became the religion of the State. But the trial of prosperity was scarcely less severe than the trial of adversity. Among the pious confessors of the reformed faith, who had been driven into banishment under Mary, bitter dissensions arose on the continent. One portion adhered at Frankfort to the ritual of the Church of England, as established by Edward; another, who had taken refuge at Geneva,

* This almost incredible fact seems to be supported by the authority of Louis XIV., who was great grandson of Philip II. Mad. Sévigné's Letters, Vol. V., p. 73, Edition of 1844.

preferred the simpler forms of worship, and the more republican system of church government, adopted by Calvin. On their return to England, after the accession of Elizabeth, these differences grew to formidable magnitude, and those inclining to the simpler forms received the name of "Puritans." The Queen leaned to the ceremonial of the ancient church; a large number of the clergy and laity regarded the ecclesiastical vestments, the use of the cross in baptism, and some other parts of the ritual, as remnants of Popery. There was no disagreement on points of doctrine; but difference of opinion and taste on these empty forms, the mere husk of religion, led to bitterness of feeling, to the formation of hostile sects (the constant scourge of Protestantism), to the interference of legislation to secure unity of worship, and when this failed, as it always has and always will, except under governments purely despotic, to the exercise of the iron arm of power to punish non-conformity. For this purpose courts of high commission and the star-chamber were established, tribunals abhorrent to the genius of the common law of England; and penalties of fine, imprisonment and death were denounced upon all whose consciences forbade them to conform to the established ritual. After various laws of greater or less severity passed for this end, the statute of 1593 was enacted, by which persevering non-conformists, guilty of no offence but that of failing to attend the Established Church, were required to abjure the realm and go into perpetual banishment;—if they did not depart within the prescribed time or returned home from exile, the penalty was death.* This atrocious statute, in its final result, peopled New England. The *fundatio perficiens*,—the real foundations of Plymouth and Massachusetts,—are to be sought not in the patent of James or the charter of Charles, with their grant of zones of territory from the Atlantic to the Pacific, but in the stern text of this act of 1593.

Its thunders slumbered at the close of the reign of Elizabeth, but not long after the accession of James the penal laws began to be executed with rigor. He had early announced that no toleration was to be extended to dissent; and in his uncouth border English had threatened to "harrie" the Puritans out of the land. That portion of them who had formally separated from the church, and were known as Brownists, were the first victims. They were driven, under circumstances of great cruelty, from England, as early as 1608, and after suffering for some years the harsh discipline of exile in Holland, went forth, the immortal band of Pilgrims, to find a new home in the wilderness. The more appropriate duties of this occasion permit us to pay only a passing tribute of respect to the precious memory of Robinson and his little flock, canonized as they are in the patriotic calendar of America, and honored in a progeny which in every State of the Union proudly traces its lineage to Plymouth Rock.

* 35 Elizabeth, c. I. See Hallam's Constitutional History, Vol. I., p. 213.

The fathers of Massachusetts belonged to the more moderate school of the Puritans. They regarded the ecclesiastical vestments and ceremonies with as little favor as the separatists; but they considered the church as established by law a true church, and still clung to her communion. But the burden lay heavy on their consciences, and at length became absolutely intolerable. Shortly after the accession of Charles I. they prepared to execute the plan which they had for some years been meditating, that of transporting themselves to the new world; where, as they supposed, they could, without a formal separation from the Church of England, adopt those simpler forms of worship and church government, which their views of divine truth required.

The waters of Massachusetts Bay, both before and after the settlement at Plymouth, had been much frequented by English fishing vessels. As early as 1619, Thompson's Island, within our limits, is known to have been occupied by an Englishman. In the year 1624, as many as fifty vessels were employed on this coast,* mostly from the West of England. Among the leading non-conformists in that quarter, none was more active and respected than Rev. John White, of Dorchester. He encouraged his parishioners and their friends to engage in these adventures, and early connected with them the idea of a gradual colonization of the coast.

---

* Dr. Young's Chronicles of Massachusetts, and the authors cited by him, page 5.

Like Robinson, in reference to Plymouth, John White never set foot upon the soil of Massachusetts, but he was the most efficient promoter of the undertaking which resulted in the settlement, not merely of our ancient town, but of the colony.

In the county of Dorset, which stretches fifty miles along the British Channel in the West of England, upon an island formed by the divided stream of "a noble river in those parts," called the Frome, lies the chief town of the county, the ancient city of Dorchester. The Britons in all probability occupied it, before the time of Julius Cæsar. Druidical mounds still surround it. The Romans, who called it *Durnovaria*, fortified it and built near it the largest Roman Amphitheatre in England, of which the circuit still remains. It was a strong-hold in the time of the Saxon Kings; the Danes stormed it; under a rapacious Norman Governor, one hundred houses, out of one hundred and eighty contained in it, were destroyed.* Every age and every race has left land-marks or ruins within its bounds; it is, by the last English census, a prosperous city of six or seven thousand inhabitants; but perhaps its most honored memorial in after times will be that it gave origin to this its American namesake, and impulse to one of the noblest enterprises of transatlantic colonization.

Of this ancient Dorchester in England, John White was the minister for well nigh forty years,

---

* Camden's Britannia, Gough's Edition, Vol. I., p. 60. The *Durotriges* are placed by Ptolemy in this region; and a British word, *Dwr*, or *Dour* (water), is supposed to be the root of their name.

being rector of the ancient church of the Trinity. Upon the life and character of this venerable man, "the Patriarch of Dorchester," as he was styled by his contemporaries; "the father of the Massachusetts Colony," as he has been called in this country, you will expect me to dwell for a moment.* He was a Puritan in principle and feeling, but not deeming the ceremonies of vital importance, he adhered to the church. But in periods of great excitement, moderation is an offence in the eyes of violent men. The cavalry of Prince Rupert sacked his house and carried off his library. This drove him to London. He was a man of most excellently tempered qualities, "grave, yet without moroseness, who would willingly contribute his shot of facetiousness on any just occasion." He was an indefatigable preacher, and "had an excellent faculty in the clear and solid interpretation of the scriptures." His executive talent was not less remarkable, and he administered the secular affairs of his church so as greatly to promote the temporal prosperity of the city. Of two things not easily controlled he had, according to Fuller, absolute command, "his own passions and the purses of his parishioners, whom he could wind up to what point he pleased on important occasions." A generous use of his own means was the secret of his command of the means of others. "He had a patriarchal influence both in Old and New England." I find no proof that this

---

* Wood's Athenæ Oxonienses: Callender's Sermon, in the Rhode Island Historical Collections, Vol. IV., 67.

influence ever ceased over the hardy young men who, by his encouragement, had settled this American Dorchester; but at home his old age was embittered by factions and the "new opinions which crept into his flock." A generation arose which slighted the crown of his old age; and of this he was "sadly and silently sensible;" sadly, as was natural in a man who had reaped ingratitude where he sowed benefits; silently, as became the self-respect of a proud, good conscience. He was one of the most learned and influential of that famous assembly of Divines at Westminster, whose catechisms, after two centuries, remain accredited manuals of Christian belief to millions on millions in the old world and the new. The biographer of the "Worthies of England," after sketching his admirable character of our ever memorable founder, expresses the hope, that Solomon's observation of the poor wise man who saved the little city, "yet no man remembered him," will not be verified of "Dorchester in England, in relation to this their deceased pastor."* He lies buried, without a stone to mark the spot, in the porch of St. Peter's church; and if the good old patriarch should be forgotten in the Dorchester of Old England, let it be some atonement to his memory, that here in New England, after a lapse of two centuries and a quarter, he is still held in pious and grateful remembrance.

Mr. White's connection with New England preceded by several years the settlement of our ancient

---

* Fuller's Worthies of England, Vol. III., p. 24, Edit. of 1840.

town. He was the chief promoter of the attempt to establish a colony at Cape Ann under Conant; and after its failure there, it was his encouragement and aid that caused the transfer of what remained of it to Salem, where it became the germ of a permanent settlement.* It was Mr. White who brought the adventurers of the West of England into connection with the men of influence in London, in Lincolnshire, and the other eastern counties, and formed with them the ever memorable company, which under a charter from Charles I., engrafted Endecott's settlement at Salem upon the languishing enterprise of the single-hearted, persevering and ill-rewarded Conant; and finally fitted out that noble expedition in 1630, under the great and good Winthrop, which put the finishing hand to the work, and consolidated the foundation of Massachusetts. In all the labors and counsels tending to this end, John White, of Dorchester, appears to have been the person of greatest activity and influence; and when all was prepared for the expedition, and the "Arbella" and her chosen company were ready to set sail, the "Humble Request," as it is called, addressed to the churches of England, setting forth, in language which can scarcely yet be read without tears, the motives and feelings which influenced the pious adventurers, is ascribed to his pen.†

* The history of the establishment at Cape Ann, illustrated with a *fac simile* of the recently recovered patent under which it was made, is given with great learning and ingenuity by John Wingate Thornton, Esq., in his late publication on this subject.

† The authorship of this paper rests upon the authority of Hubbard, who speaks of it as a thing "commonly said." This must be considered good

With us, fellow citizens of Dorchester, his connection is still more intimate. There was a large body of "West Country," or "Dorchester men," in Gov. Winthrop's expedition, who were many of them of Mr. White's church, and all were enlisted, so to say, under his auspices and encouragement; and they were the first in the field. Early in March, 1630, they were ready to depart, and a large vessel was chartered at Plymouth, for their separate conveyance. The faithful pastor, guide at once in things divine and human—which in that age of trial ran strangely together, as in what age do they not?—went with them to their port of embarkation; met with them in the New Hospital at Plymouth, where they gathered themselves into a church under the ministers of his selection; held with them a solemn fast of preparation, and preached to them the last sermon they were to hear from his lips:—

——prompt at every call,
He watched and wept, he prayed and felt for all.

And so on the 20th March, 1630, the Dorchester emigrants embarked in the Mary and John, Capt. Squeb master, a vessel of 400 tons. They had a prosperous voyage of seventy days, and arrived at Nantasket on the 30th of May, about ten days in advance of the "Arbella," and the vessels which accompanied her. The Dorchester company contained

---

evidence that such was the tradition in his time. Dr. Young thinks it more likely that the "Humble Request" was written by Winthrop or Johnson (Chronicles of Mass., p. 299); but as its chief object was to define the relation of the adventurers to the Established Church, it appears to me more likely to have been written by a clergyman. Prince adopts Hubbard's tradition (Chronology, p. 275).

several persons of consideration and substance, a numerous party of emigrants with their wives and children, and a frugal store of worldly goods. They were attended by their pastors Messrs. Maverick and Warham,—by whom, says Roger Clap, in his narrative of the voyage, "we had preaching or expounding of the word of God every day for ten weeks together."

Capt. Squeb was under engagement to convey the company to Charles River, but by a latitude of interpretation not peculiar to him, and not perhaps strange at a time when the localities were so little understood, he insisted, greatly to their discontent, on landing them and their cattle at Nantasket. This spot furnished no room nor other facilities for the proposed new settlement, besides being already occupied by "Old Planters" as they were called ("old" on the coast of Massachusetts in 1630!); that is, individuals who had separated themselves from the other independent settlements such as those of Plymouth, Cape Ann, Weymouth, or Salem, or had found their way in the fishing vessels to these coasts. From one of these old planters, a boat was borrowed by the newly arrived company, and a party of ten, headed by brave Capt. Southcoat, who had served in the low countries, was sent up to explore Charles River in search of a place for a settlement. Roger Clap was one of this party;—they went up the river as far as Watertown, passed a day or two on a spot near the present arsenal, and still called "Dorchester fields," and held friendly communications with the Indians of that place, which afterwards became the first field of the apostolic labors of Eliot, who, when he was in the flesh, sat in the chair in which you, Sir (Gov. Gardner), now sit. The main body meantime had explored the coast nearer Nantasket, and having found "a neck of land fit to keep their cattle on," called Mattapan, had established themselves there.* This, after some hesitation, was adopted as the permanent seat of the settlement.

This "neck of land" was the present South Boston, which within my recollection was still called Dorchester neck. The curving bay, which sweeps round between the neck and Savin hill, still bears on our maps the name of "Old Harbor," and the rising grounds to the South were the site of the first habitations. The first humble meeting-house with its thatched roof,—which caught a year or two afterwards as Mr. Maverick the minister was "drying a little powder (which took fire by the heat of the firepan"),—it being one of the first cares of the puritan fathers to keep their powder dry,—stood probably at the northern end of the plain, now called Pleasant street; and close by its side,—somewhat to the north-east of the present ancient cemetery,—was the first place of burial, of which no traces now remain. It was at first supposed that Dorchester might become the emporium of the new colony. Capt. Smith, in his rude map of the coast, had placed the name of "London" on the spot afterwards and still called Squantum, and a fort was

* The facts relative to the organization of the Dorchester Church at Plymouth, the voyage, and the settlement at Mattapan, are recorded in Roger Clap's Memoir.

built on Savin hill, and a battery on the shore, for the protection of the future metropolis. It soon appeared, however, that the water was not of sufficient depth for this purpose, and Boston was ascertained to be the spot marked out by nature as the future capital of New England. On the 17th of September, 1630, at a meeting of the Court of Assistants at Charlestown, which had already received that name, it was "ordered that Trimountaine shall be called Boston; Mattapan Dorchester; and the towne vpon Charles Ryver Waterton." *

Such, fellow citizens, in the plainest language in which I can relate it, is the simple tale of the foundation of Dorchester, which preceded by a short time the settlements made by the main body of Gov. Winthrop's party at the other towns just named. The hardships of the entire emigration were for the first season severe. They were disappointed in the expectation of deriving supplies from the settlers at Salem; there was dearth there. The stock of provisions brought from England was inadequate for the support of so large a company, and it was too late in the year to plant; the diseases sure to be engendered by want and anxiety prevailed; the native tribes in the neighborhood were an object of exaggerated though natural terror; alarms of invasion from the French and Dutch penetrated to these remote corners of the earth; and the hearts of some failed them

---

* Massachusetts Records, Vol. I., p. 75. I quote, of course, the recently published edition of the Records, superintended and prepared with extreme accuracy by Dr. Nath'l B. Shurtleff, and printed in a style of unsurpassed beauty at the expense of the Commonwealth.

at the thoughts of their distant home, as want stared them in the face. "In our beginnings," says Roger Clap, "many were in great straights for want of provisions for themselves and little ones. Oh! the hunger that many suffered and saw no hope in an eye of reason to be supplied, only by clams, muscles, and fish."

With all our contemporary accounts and traditions, I imagine we form very inadequate conceptions of the hardships endured by the first settlers of this country. Modern art, with its various astonishing applications, traverses the ocean on its chariot wheels of fire, and transports the traveller in ten or twelve days from Europe to America. Even the sailing vessels accomplish the voyage in three or four weeks. The passages in the seventeenth century were more frequently of two or three months' duration. The Mary and John, without having met with any disaster, was out seventy days. Modern enterprise encounters the expected navigators at sea; sends out her pilot-boat, bounding like a sea-bird on the waves, a hundred miles from port (who that has witnessed the sight homeward bound will ever forget it); unrols her charts, where every shoal and rock is projected, and the soundings laid down so carefully, that you may find your way in the dark, studs the coast with light-houses, and receives the weather-beaten ship at convenient landing places. The first settlers were obliged to feel their way into unknown harbors, ignorant of the depths and shallows, the rocks and the currents, often finding the greatest discomforts and dangers of the voyage awaiting them at its close.*

Nor were the difficulties less after landing. The "state of nature" in which they found the country, "bare creation" as it is expressively called by an early writer (Dummer), the goal of their wishes and prayers, was a far different thing from that which presents itself to the mind, when those words are used by us. Few, I fear, even in this intelligent audience, have formed an adequate notion of the hard rough nature that confronted our fathers, two centuries and a quarter ago, on these now delightful spots. The "nature" which we think of consists of dreamy lawns, dotted here and there with picturesque cottages, hung with festoons of prairie-rose and honey-suckle;—of shady walks, winding through groves carefully cleared of the thorns and brambles, that weave its matted underbrush into an impenetrable thicket;—of grand sea-views from the cool porticoes of marine villas;—of glimpses of babbling streams as they sparkle through meadows, vocal with lowing herds and bleating flocks. This we call nature, and so it is; but it is nature brought into loving union with the skilful hand and tasteful eye of man, the great "minister and interpreter of nature." Great heavens! how different the nature which frowned upon the fathers and mothers of New England;—harsh, austere, wearisome, often terrific.

* This is well illustrated in the voyage of the Rev. Richard Mather, the first pastor of Dorchester after the re-organization of the church in 1636.—Collections of Dorchester Antiquarian and Historical Society, No. III.

On the sea-board, broad marshes cut up with deep oozy creeks, and unfordable tide-water rivers,—no dykes, no bridges, no roads, no works of friendly communication of any kind;—in short, no traces of humanity in the kindly structures for travel, shelter, neighborhood, or defence, which raise the homes of man above the lairs of wild beasts. In fact, the aboriginal tribes, in this respect, hardly went as far as the beavers, who in their small way were very tolerable engineers for wet meadows.

Such was the coast; as you retreated from it, you entered the terrific wilderness, which stretched from ocean to ocean, the abode of the savage and the wild beast,—gloomy—awful! No civilized foot had penetrated its depths,—no surveyor's chain had measured its boundaries,—no Christian eye had searched its dismal shades. In the ignorance that prevailed as to the real character of the new and unexplored country, imagination naturally added fictitious to real terrors. Unearthly cries were sometimes heard in the crackling woods; glimpses were caught, at dusk, of animals, for which natural history had no names; and strange foot-marks which men did not like to speak of, were occasionally seen in the snow. Even amidst the multiplying settlements, the hill-sides were alive with rattle-snakes, a reptile unknown and much dreaded in Europe; and the ravening bear and wolf were heard by night around the farm-yard. Humanity lost the kindly links of intelligible language; and was seen only under the aspect of a strange race, whose numbers and strength were unknown, and whose disposition toward the new comers remained to be learned from experience.

But these hardships and terrors yielded to the courage and perseverance of our fathers, and the all-subduing power of time. Dorchester, with the usual vicissitudes of a new country, prospered. As it was by a slight priority the first town settled by Governor Winthrop's party, it retained for a short time a certain precedence. In 1633, a tax of four hundred pounds was laid, of which Dorchester paid eighty pounds,—Boston, Roxbury, Newtown (afterwards Cambridge), Watertown, and Charlestown, paid £48 each, Saugus £36, Salem £28, and Medford £12; and these were the whole of Massachusetts, two centuries and a quarter ago! In the year 1633, Wood calls our ancient town "the greatest town in New England." The description of Josselyn is still more glowing. Its geographical extent, till reduced by the separation from it of several large new towns, was great. It comprised the modern towns of Milton, Stoughton, Sharon, Canton, and Foxborough, with a part of Wrentham and Dedham, being of the length of thirty-five miles, and the average breadth of five. Nor was it merely in time or wealth that it took for a short time the lead. It set the example, in 1633, of that municipal organization which has prevailed throughout New England, and has proved one of the chief sources of its progress. It has been supposed that the first stated provision for a public school was made here:—but the loss of the earliest leaves of our town records leaves us without the documentary proof of this fact, if it be one.

One would suppose that the extensive territory I have just described, would have afforded ample accommodation for some two or three hundred inhabitants. They had, however, scarcely established themselves in their new home, before they began to be straightened for want of room. It seems to have been thought extremely desirable, in the first settlement of the country, to be seated either on the sea coast or the banks of a river. The inhabitants of the Bay had been early made acquainted by those at Plymouth with Connecticut River, although the court declined an application from that quarter, to join them in anticipating the Dutch in their attempts to get possession of it. Three or four individuals, however, from Dorchester, had as early as 1633 crossed the intervening wilderness, and explored this magnificent stream.

Influenced by their reports of the noble range of pasturage to be found on its banks, aided, it must be confessed, by discontents in the Bay, an emigration was contemplated in 1634 by the inhabitants of Dorchester and Newtown. Mr. Ludlow, of Dorchester, it was said, thought that some other persons, himself included, would fill the chair of State as well as Governor Winthrop; and the star of Mr. Hooker in the church at Newtown, it was thought, was not wanted so near the light of John Cotton. The emigration was warmly debated in the Court. Fifteen out of twenty-five of the infant house of deputies, first elected that year, were for the removal; a majority of the magistrates placed their *veto* on the measure, and great heats ensued.

It was opposed on various grounds, but the "procatarctical" reason (as Hubbard somewhat learnedly expresses it) was, that so many of its inhabitants could not safely be spared from the Bay.* The next year the Rev. Messrs. Richard Mather, and Thomas Shepherd, with numerous associates, arrived in the colony. Mr. Mather's company being prepared to fill the places of those desiring to leave Dorchester, and Mr. Shepherd's to succeed to their brethren at Newtown ([illegible]), the Court gave way and permitted the undertaking. A portion of the emigrants went in the autumn of 1635, the residue in the following spring. Great were the hardships and severe the sufferings endured in this early American exodus through the wilderness, first faint image of that living tide of emigration which in all subsequent time has flowed westward from the Atlantic coast, till in our day it has reached the boundless west; and is even now swelling over the Rocky Mountains, and spreading itself on the shores of the Pacific. Still may it swell and still may it flow; bearing upon its bosom the laws and the institutions, the letters and the arts, the freedom and the faith, which have given New England her name and praise in the world! † The adventurers from Dorchester,—men, women and children,—were fourteen days in making the journey now daily accomplished in three hours, and reached the river

* Winthrop's Journal for 4th September, 1634.

† This emigration is beautifully described in the Life of John Mason, by Rev. George E. Ellis; Sparks's Library of American Biography, Vol. XIII., p. 331.

weak with toil and hunger, and all but disheartened. Both the Dorchester ministers, though it is said reluctantly, agreed to join their emigrating church. Mr. Maverick the senior died in Boston before starting; Mr. Warham conducted his flock to East Windsor, where they formed the first church in Connecticut, as they had been in Massachusetts second to Salem alone. Thus from our native town of Dorchester, and from Cambridge, not yet bearing that honored name, within five years from their first settlement, went forth the founders of Connecticut.

Nor was it for their own establishment alone that the early fathers of Dorchester were careful; they remembered the native children of the soil with kindness. When, a few years after the emigration to the Connecticut, the increase of the new comers about the falls of Neponset had begun to press hard upon the natives gathered about that spot, on the application of John Eliot a grant of six thousand acres of land, being the greater part of the modern town of Stoughton, was made by Dorchester for their accommodation; a grant, as one of our town clerks well says, without example in the history of the State.* In this pleasant retreat were collected the remnants of the friendly tribe, who gave us this venerable name of MASSACHUSETTS, and who ruled the shores of the noble BAY, which, in years past, added another epithet to this time-honored designation. The fair domain of this, our name-sake tribe,

* Noah Clap's letter, 4 Jan., 1792. Mass. Hist. Coll., First Series, Vol. I., p. 98.

extended from the broad smooth floor of Nantasket, where the whispering ripple, as it runs up the beach, scarcely effaces the foot prints of the smart little sand-piper, all round to the cold gray ledges of Nahant, on which the mountain waves of the Atlantic, broken and tired with their tempestuous weltering march through seventy degrees of longitude, conflicting with all the winds of Heaven, sink down upon their adamantine bed, like weary Titans after battling with the gods, and lulled by the moaning dirges of their voiceful caves, roll and rock themselves heavily to sleep. Some "old men of Massachusetts" affirmed that in the interior they extended as far west as Pocomtacook. They hunted small game in the blue-hills, and on their snow-shoes they followed the deer to Wachusett. They passed in their bark canoes through Mother Brook into Charles River; the falls of Nonantum and the head waters of the Mystic were favorite resorts; they ranged even to the Nashua. Their war parties met the Tarratines on the Shawshine and the Merrimac;—but they loved especially the fair headland of Squantum; the centre of their power was Neponset falls.

From the origin of the colony they were the friends of the white man, and in the first mention of Mattapan as the place of the future settlement, it is stated, that "there also the Indians were kind to us." Thinned by a pestilential disease before the arrival of the English, overshadowed by the numbers, the physical power, and the intellectual superiority of the new comer, reading in the events of every day the terrible but inevitable doom, "he must increase, but I must decrease," they adopted the white man's faith, and by a miracle of Christian pains and charity read the white man's Book in their native tongue. But not even that mighty element of life, to which the civilized nations of the earth owe so much of their vitality, availed to prolong the red man's existence. Twelve families only of praying Indians, as they were called, the remains of those who removed from Neponset, were found by Gookin at Punkapoag in 1674.* John Eliot, jun., the son of the apostle,—and truly I know not who, since Peter and Paul, better deserves that name,—labored with them once a fortnight. But they dwindled with each generation; till in my boyhood I remember hearing of one poor solitary Indian, who, it was said, occupied a lonely wigwam on Stoughton Pond, and who used to come down, once or twice a year, to the sea-side; hovered a day or two about Squantum; caught a few fish at the lower mills; strolled off into the woods, and with plaintive wailings cut away the bushes from an ancient mound, which, as he thought, covered the ashes of his fathers; and then went back a silent, broken, melancholy man,—the last of a perished tribe.

The agency of Dorchester in the settlement of Connecticut is not the only incident of the kind in our annals. Two generations later, viz., in 1695, application was made to our minister, Mr. Danforth,

---

* Mass. Hist. Collections, First Series, Vol. I., p. 184.

both personally and by letter, from South Carolina, setting forth the spiritual destitution of that region, and asking aid from us. A missionary church was forthwith organized, in compliance with this request from the remote sister plantation. A pastor, Mr. Joseph Lord, was ordained over it;—it sailed from Dorchester in the middle of December, and arrived at its destination in fourteen days. The little community established itself on Ashley river, in South Carolina, and fondly assumed the name of Dorchester. Here, for more than half a century, the transplanted church and settlement enjoyed a modest prosperity. But the situation proving unhealthy, and the quantity of land limited, a removal to Georgia was projected in 1752. The legislature of that colony made a liberal grant of land, where the emigrants from Dorchester founded the town of Midway, as being half-way between the rivers Ogeechee and Altamaha. This settlement constituted a considerable part of the parish of St. John's, afterwards honorably known as Liberty County in Georgia. Its inhabitants, in the third generation, retained the character and manners, the feelings and principles, which their ancestors brought from our Dorchester eighty years before. On the assembling of the Continental Congress at Philadelphia in 1774, Georgia as a colony not having chosen delegates, the parish of St. John's addressed themselves directly to that body, and received from them a copy of the "General Association." The Convention of Georgia declining to join it without modification, the Parish of St. John's subscribed it on their own account, and sent one of their number, Dr. Lyman Hall, a native of Connecticut, a member of the little Dorchester-Midway church, to represent that Parish in the Congress at Philadelphia. "At this period," says Dr. Stevens, the intelligent historian of Georgia, "the parish of St. John's possessed nearly one third of the entire wealth of the province; and its inhabitants were remarkable for their upright and independent character. Sympathizing, from their New England origin, more strongly with the northern distresses than the other parts of Georgia, and being removed from the immediate supervision of the Governor and his Council, they pressed on with greater ardor and a firmer step than her sister parishes. The time for action had arrived, and the irresolution of fear had no place in their decisive councils. Alone she stood, a Pharos of liberty in England's most loyal province, renouncing every fellowship that savored not of freedom, and refusing every luxury which contributed to ministerial coffers. With a halter around her neck and a gallows before her eyes, she severed herself from surrounding associations, and cast her lot, while as yet all was gloom and darkness, with the fortunes of her country, to live with her rights or to die for their defence. Proud spot of Georgia's soil! Well does it deserve the appellation (Liberty County) which a grateful State conferred upon it; and truly may we say of its sons, in the remembrance of their patriotic services, "nothing was wanting to their glory, they were wanting to ours."*

---

* Georgia Historical Collections, Vol. II., p. 24.

Dr. Hall appeared at Philadelphia on the third day of the session of 1775 (13th May), and was admitted as a delegate. On that day Congress was composed of the representatives of the twelve United Colonies, and Dr. Lyman Hall, the deputy from the Parish of St. John's. The patriotic example was soon followed by the colony, and four delegates, of whom Dr. Hall was one, were in the course of a few weeks deputed to Philadelphia. In this way, and by the strange sequence of events which pervades our history, the pious zeal of a few humble Christians of our ancient town, in 1695, was the remote cause that the great empire State of the South, then in its infancy, was represented at the opening of the Congress of 1775. A deputation from this distant offshoot of the old Dorchester stock has been expected to favor us with their attendance on this occasion. If they are present, we bid them cordially welcome.*

It cannot be expected that the annals of a small municipality like Dorchester should furnish many events of striking public interest. It is enough to say of our fathers that they bore their part faithfully in the silent work of progress, which was carried on under both charters. Among them were many individuals of great worth, and some who have played a distinguished part in public affairs.

Of Maverick and Warham, the first ministers, not

---

* This interesting and important incident in the History of Dorchester is fully narrated by the Rev. Dr. Holmes, who in early life was the pastor of the Midway church. See *Annals*, under the years 1696, and 1775. Also Journals of the Continental Congress for 13th May, 1775.

much is known. Warham had been the clergyman of Exeter in England, and they were both selected by Mr. White as the spiritual guides (and that imported little less than a moral dictatorship) of the infant colony. His name is still perpetuated in Connecticut.

When their services were lost to the church of Dorchester, by the decease of Mr. Maverick in 1636 and the emigration of Mr. Warham to Connecticut, their place was more than filled by Mr. Richard Mather, the leader of the second emigration, a person of great authority in the infant churches of the colony, the father of Increase Mather, the grandfather of Cotton Mather, and as such the head of a family which for nearly a century filled no second place in the church of New England.

Mr. Rossiter was one of the assistants chosen in London in 1629, but died in a short time after his arrival.

Mr. Ludlow, also one of the first emigration, was of the magistracy in 1630; deputy in 1634, and an unsuccessful candidate for the governorship the next year. He was unwise enough to let this want of success disturb his equanimity, and protested against the election of Winthrop. The constituency were offended at this, and refused to continue him in the second office. In the gentle phrase of Dr. Eliot, they "gave him an opportunity to enjoy private life." Disgusted with the turn things were taking in the Bay, he joined the emigration to Connecticut, and took a distinguished part in the affairs of that colony. He finally removed to Virginia.

I have already spoken of Roger Clap, whose diary relates the voyage and settlement of the first company of Dorchester emigrants, and is an interesting original contribution to our early history. Induced by his example and advice, several of his kindred followed him to America, among whose descendants are those of that name, who in every generation have creditably served their native town, as well as some of the most eminent sons of New England in other parts of the country. Of this stock was the learned President Clap of Yale College, and the venerable Nathanael Clap of Newport, of whom Bishop Berkeley said, "before I saw Father Clap, I thought the Bishop of Rome (Pope Clement XI.) had the most grave aspect of any man I ever saw, but really the minister of Newport has the most venerable appearance. The resemblance is very great." I may be permitted to allude to my own grateful associations with this name, as that of the patient and faithful instructress of the same lineage, who taught me to read before I could speak plain. Considerately mingling the teacher and nurse, she kept a pillow and a bit of carpet in the corner of the school-room, where the little heads, throbbing from a premature struggle with the tall double letters and ampersand, with Korah's troop and Vashti's pride, were permitted, nay encouraged, to go to sleep. Roger Clap was a military man; and in time succeeded, with the title of Captain, to the command of our stout little colonial Sebastopol,—originally the Castle, then Castle William, and now Fort Independence:—a fortress coeval with the colony; whose walls first of mud, then of wood, then of brick, and now lastly of granite, not inappropriately symbolize the successive stages of our political growth. When the great Dutch Admiral de Ruyter, the year after that famous *Annus Mirabilis* immortalized by Dryden, having swept the coast of Africa had been ordered to the West Indies, intending, says Capt. Clap, not a whit daunted at the thought, "to visit us," the Captain adds, with honest satisfaction, "Our battery was also repaired, wherein are seven good guns," probably six pounders at least. De Ruyter, however, did not think it expedient to come within two thousand miles of their range.

John Mason was a chieftain of still greater eminence. He had served under Fairfax in the low countries. He commanded the Dorchester train band in 1633, but led the emigration three years afterwards to Connecticut. When the great Pequot war broke out, he commanded the river troops; and at the famous battle of the Mystic, in May 1637, he all but annihilated that hostile tribe. He was among the most active, useful, and honored of the Dorchester company, and of the founders of Connecticut; whose fate depended for the time on the success of the battle of the Mystic. The late Jeremiah Mason, one of the most distinguished of the statesmen and jurists of our own time, was among his descendants.

William Pynchon early removed from Dorchester to Roxbury, and thence to Springfield,—the most prominent of the founders of Western Massachusetts.

Israel Stoughton was probably one of the first emigration; his name appears on one of the earliest pages of our Dorchester annals. He was a member of the first general court of deputies; a citizen of energy and public spirit. Unlike modern legislators, who, "without distinction of party," are accused of looking out for the loaves and fishes for themselves, worthy Col. Stoughton provided them for others. He built the first tide-mill for grinding corn, and established the first wier for taking fish in the colony. He, too, was a military man, and commanded the contingent from Massachusetts in the Pequot war. After filling important trusts in New England, he returned home and served as a colonel in the parliamentary army. By his will he bequeathed three hundred acres of land to Harvard College.

His son William fills a still more distinguished place in the history of Dorchester and Massachusetts. He was educated for the pulpit, and often urged to settle over the church of his native town and elsewhere. He preached the annual election sermon in 1668, from which one striking expression is still remembered: "God sifted a whole nation that he might send choice grain over into this wilderness." He was an agent for the colony at the court of Charles II., and was afterwards named Deputy Governor in the new charter, subsequently acting as chief magistrate on the departure of Phipps and Bellamont. He built a college at Cambridge, which bore his name;—a memorial of his liberality which has been perpetuated by a college edifice, of more recent construction, but bearing the same name. His monument, the most costly in our ancient burial ground, the work probably of a foreign artist, is conspicuous for a highly rhetorical inscription, of which the material portion is borrowed from that of Pascal.

William Poole was of the first company of emigrants, for several years town clerk and school-master. He lived a considerable time at Taunton, where the benefactions of his sister procured for her the honorable title of the "Virgin Mother" of that town. William Poole is spoken of in our records as a "sage, reverend, and pious man of God." His epitaph, written by himself before his death, is still legible upon his grave stone, and is one of the best expressed of our mortuary inscriptions:

"Ho paſsenger tis worth thy paines to ſtay
& take a dead mans leſson by ye way
I was what now thou art & thou ſhalt be
what I am now what odds twixt me & thee
Now go thy way but ſtay take one word more
Thy ſtaff, for ought thou knowest, stands next ye dore
Death is ye dore ye dore of heaven or hell
Be warned, Be armed Beliue Repent Fariewell."

Edmund Hartt is just mentioned in the list of the first company. I suppose him to be the ancestor of Edmund Hartt who built the frigate "Constitution." It has been denied that he drew the plan of that noble ship; doubted even if he superintended the work; but he was at least the "master" who "laid the keel;" and the master who laid the keel of "Old Ironsides," even if he worked with no higher instruments than mallet and chisel, was surely a workman that needeth not to be ashamed of his work, nor Dorchester of the workman.

Robert Pierce was of the first emigration, and was the ancestor of the late venerable and beloved Dr. Pierce of Brookline. He built the house in which one of his descendants, Mr. Lewis Pierce, lives at the present day, in whose possession is still preserved a portion of the bread brought from England by his ancestor; a "remainder biscuit" certainly, and by this time a pretty dry one.*

Humphrey Atherton was of the second emigration, a man of mark and influence in the colony. He filled some of the most important offices of civil life, and attained the highest military rank. He was "slow of speech;" but "downright for the business, one of cheerful spirit and entire for the country." After having been employed on almost every occasion of importance, in peace or war, for thirty years, he was thrown from his horse as he was riding from Boston, and killed. His death (in 1661) was regarded as a public calamity. The sensation caused by it has been handed down to posterity in the monumental record, still legible upon his tomb-stone, and still constantly quoted, in which, at some expense of grammar and rhythm, the high qualities of his character and the pomp of his obsequies are set forth with a certain solemn quaintness not unpleasing to a native Dorchester ear:

"Here lies ovr Captaine, & Major of Svffolk was withall;
A Godly Majiftrate was he, and Maior Generall,

---

* Mr. Everett here exhibited in a glass case two sea-biscuits which were brought over by Mr. Robert Pierce, and have been carefully preserved in his family to the present day.

Two Trovps of Hors with him heare came, ſvch worth his love
did crave;
Ten Companyes of Foot also movrning marcht to his grave.
Let all that Read be ſure to keep the Faith as he has don
With Chriſt he lives now Crown'd his name was Hvmpry Atherton."

But time would fail me to mention even by name all the persons entitled to a respectful recollection in our history. It is enough to say that they comprehend a fair proportion of the eminent men of the colony, and that a large number of those most distinguished in New England, or the States settled from New England, trace their origin directly or collaterally to this spot. In proof of this assertion, besides the names already given, I might repeat those of Roger Sherman, Strong, Dewey, Wolcott, Hawthorne, Putnam, Phillips, Breck, Minot, Moseley, Withington, Robinson, and many others. So, too, it would be easy to show, from the contents of our ancient records, if the limits of the occasion permitted it, that the character of Dorchester, as a town, was at all times sustained upon the solid basis on which the fathers had placed it. When we bear in mind the great power and influence of the church in the early days, as a species of moral and spiritual government, outside and above the municipal organization, and exercising a paramount control far beyond the strict bounds of ecclesiastical affairs, we shall be prepared to admit, that the steadiness of our progress and the general prosperity which the town has enjoyed, are owing, in no small degree, to the diligent labors, faithful services, and excellent characters of its clergy, an unbroken line of pious, learned, and devoted men. The whole period, from the emigration to Connecticut in 1636 to the resignation of Mr. Bowman in 1773, is covered by the lives of Mather, Flint, Danforth, and Bowman, who with Messrs. Burr and Wilson, both colleagues of Mather, make up the list. It would not become me to speak of Mr. Bowman's successor, a near relative of my own; while the memory of Dr. Harris, the last pastor of the first, and of Dr. Codman, the first pastor of the second Dorchester church, is too recent to require a tribute. It would not perhaps be easy to find a town, which has been more highly favored in a succession of ministers modelled upon the true type of a New England Pastor, in whom a well-digested store of human and divine learning, directed by a sound practical judgment, was united with an all-controlling sense of the worth of spiritual things; while the austerity of manners required by the taste of the age was sustained by spotless purity of life, and habitually softened by offices of charity and words of love. Notwithstanding the dissensions with which the churches of New England, in the course of two centuries, were too often agitated, and the consequent frequent disturbance of the friendly relations of Minister and People, I do not know that there is one of the Ministers of Dorchester who may not be considered as having adorned his office, and as having exercised a kindly and healing influence on the church and the community.

With respect to the great reproach of our puritan fathers, that of intolerance, too well founded as we must all admit and lament, I cannot find that our ancient town was above or below the standard of the age. It was an age which sincerely believed itself in direct alliance with the Supreme Being. The Colonial government for two generations had all the essential features of a theocracy. Every event, from the sickness or death of the minister of a village church, to that of a foreign potentate, a winter's storm or a summer's drought, canker worms in the spring and frosts in the autumn, a heresy invading the church, a *quo warranto* threatening the charter, an Indian or a European war, was the occasion of a fast, and "improved" in a spiritual application. We use the same language as our forefathers in this respect. The difference between us and them, I fear, is, that they believed what they said, with a more profound conviction. But while their lofty faith gave a high tone to their characters, its influence was not in all respects favorable to the happiness of their lives, the wisdom of their counsels, or the charity of their opinions. Our poor natures are not strong enough to bear a direct personal union with the Infinite. We are too prone to do wrong, to be trusted with the consciousness of infallibility; too ignorant, to be safely animated with the conviction that we have grasped the whole truth. The annals of Dorchester, however, present a few noble examples of charity and toleration beyond the age. When the statute against the Quakers was enacted in 1658, a statute which reproduced the worst features of the cruel law against non-conformists of 1593, Thomas Clark, with one other deputy, voted against it. He was a Dorchester man, though removed to Boston, which he represented at that time;—and Nicholas Upsall, also of Dorchester, was fined, imprisoned, and eventually banished, for deeds of mercy toward that persecuted sect.

In all the important political events of the times, the town of Dorchester bore its part, often a conspicuous one. A very striking illustration of this fact may be seen in the Memorial addressed to the Colonial legislature in 1664, and signed by the principal inhabitants of the town.* The New England Colonies, though by no means what can be called a military people, had been led by circumstances to a large experience of the hardships and perils of war. This grew at first out of the necessity of protecting themselves against the native tribes; which they were obliged to do, entirely without aid from the mother country. I do not recollect that, under the first charter, a dollar or a man was sent from England to the Colonies, to aid in their defence against the Indians, the French, or the Dutch. Under the new charter, and with the increase of population both in the French and British Colonies, American interests acquired a greatly increased importance; and the Colonies, as a matter of course, were involved in all the wars of Europe. A considerable military and naval force was always kept up, and the royal navies and armies were recruited for foreign service in New England. In this way, the flower of our youth, for three successive genera-

* This interesting paper was published in the New England Genealogical Register, Vol. V., p. 393, with valuable notices of the signers.

tions, were engaged in a series of sanguinary but now almost forgotten conflicts on the inland frontier, the banks of the St. Lawrence, in Cape Breton, in Martinico and Cuba, and on the Spanish Main. Besides what was done still earlier, the New England Colonies raised two thousand men in 1690 for that fatal expedition against Canada, of whom one thousand perished, "not vagrants," says Dummer, "picked up in the streets and pressed into the war, but heads of families, artificers, robust young men, such as no country can spare, and least of all, new settlements."* Expeditions of this kind, sometimes prosperous, more frequently attended with the most distressing sacrifices, not merely of property but of life, recur too frequently even to be enumerated here. I mention only those which are alluded to in our histories. In 1740, five companies of one hundred men each, as the excellent Mr. James Blake, for so many years the faithful town clerk of Dorchester, relates, "went from this province to war with Spain. They went to Jamaica to Admiral Vernon, and so to Carthagena and Cuba." Mr. Blake adds, "we hear many or most of them are dead." Let us hope that the town clerk of Dorchester will never again have to make precisely that record. Three thousand men were raised in New England for the memorable expedition against Louisburg in 1745. "Most that went from hereabouts," says Father Blake, "that I knew, either died there, or in their passage home, or soon after they came

* Defence of the New England Charters, p. 17.

home. 'Tis said there died of our New England forces about five hundred." This expedition, as you are well aware, was planned by Gov. Shirley. The Governor's stately mansion still stands upon our borders; the iron cross, brought from the market-place at Louisburg, adorns the library of Harvard College. But no monument is reared to the brave men who fell in these distant expeditions; no memorial remains of those who came back to their native villages, with wounds and diseases brought from the camp. On one mouldering stone only, in our ancient grave-yard, we read that it covers a person who "died in his majesty's sarvice."

> The Indian's shaft, the Briton's ball,
> The sabre's thirsting edge,
> The hot-shell shattering in its fall,
> The bayonet's rending wedge
> There scattered death;—yet seek the spot,
> No trace thine eye can see,
> No altar; and they need it not,
> Who leave their children free.*

The great expedition against the Havana, in 1762, was on the point of sinking under the climate and the protracted resistance of the Spaniards. "A thousand languishing and impatient looks," says the historian, "were cast *on the reinforcements from America.*" None, however, as yet appeared; and the exhausted army was left to its own resources. Many fell into despair and died, overcome with fatigue, anguish, and disappointment. These reinforcements at length arrived in two divisions. Some

---

* Holmes.

of the vessels composing the first, were wrecked in the Bahama passage; of the second, a part were intercepted by the French; but those who escaped, "arrived seasonably and rendered excellent service." On the 14th day of August, 1762, after a murderous siege of two months and eight days, under a burning tropical sun, in mid-summer, the Royal forces of England, with her brave provincial allies, marched together through the battered wall of the Havana.* This was an era in history; it was the last time in which England and her North American colonies stood side by side on the battle field. Their next meetings were fifteen years later at Lexington and Concord, at Bunker Hill and Dorchester heights;— No, not on Dorchester heights; it was not deemed expedient by the royal forces to meet them there.

In 1763, the temple of Janus was shut, and there was peace throughout christendom. England had gained an empire in the war; Canada had been acquired by her, and, with her elder American colonies, spread out before her one vast field for the promotion of human happiness and the culture of a high civilization. By the hand of Chatham she might have sown protection, and reaped grateful allegiance. From the lips of Burke she might have sown conciliation, and reaped union and love. But by the counsels of Grenville and North she sowed taxation, and reaped revolt. In 1764 she sowed the wind (a crop which never comes up in regular drills); she came for the harvest in 1775, and, lo! the whirl-

* Annual Register for 1762, chap. VIII.

wind; reaper, sickle, and sheaves swept before the tempest; the fountains of the great deep broken up; and the very soil itself, the rock-ribbed continent, torn from the British empire by the convulsion!

In the struggle, which began with the passage of the Stamp-act, Dorchester was in no degree behind the metropolis. In 1765 she instructed her representative, Col. John Robinson, "to use the utmost of his endeavors, with the great and general court, to obtain the repeal of the late parliamentary act, (always earnestly asserting our rights as free-born Englishmen), and his best skill in preventing the use of stamped paper in this government." But though resolutely bent on resisting the obnoxious and tyrannical act, they would nevertheless manifest to him their "utter abhorrence of all routs, riots, tumults, and unlawful assemblies; and if the laws now in being are not sufficient to suppress such high misdemeanors, that you would use your skill and interest in making such laws as would answer such a salutary purpose." (Dorchester Rec. III., 293.) When, in consequence of the dissolution of the general court in 1768, a convention of the Province was recommended by Boston, Dorchester voted "to choose one person to act as a committee in convention, with such committee as may be sent from other towns in the province, in order that such measures may be consulted and advised, as his majesty's service and the peace and safety of his subjects in this province may require." As a farther measure to promote his majesty's service and the peace and safety of the province, the next vote passed at the same meeting was, that a "place be built under the roof of the meeting-house at the east end thereof, to keep the town's stock of powder in." (Rec. III., 333.) In 1770, Dorchester resolved not to purchase any articles of the traders in Boston, who had violated the non-importation agreement, and resolved that "whereas a duty has been laid on foreign tea, we will not make use of it in our families, except in case of sickness, till the duty is repealed." (Rec. III., 352.) On the 4th of June, 1773, Dorchester responded to the solemn exposition of the rights of America, drawn up by a committee of twenty-one of the citizens of Boston. The resolutions of this town were nine in number, expressed with perspicuity and force, and the representatives of Dorchester are instructed "to join in any motion or motions in a constitutional way, to obtain not only redress of the aforementioned grievances, but of all others, and that they in no wise consent to give up any of our rights, whether from nature or by compact." (Rec. III., 380.)

At the close of 1773, the great question of taxation, out of which sprung the independence of America, was brought to a practical issue in reference to the duty on tea. When attempts were made to persuade Lord North not to introduce the obnoxious article into the colonies, his answer was, "It is of no use making objections, for the King will have it so. The King means to try the question"; and the question was tried in Boston and its vicinity.* As soon as information was received that

* Bancroft's History, Vol. VI., p. 465, 472.

two or three cargoes of tea were speedily to arrive in Boston, the consignees were called upon, by a committee of the citizens in town meeting assembled, to resign their trust. This they refused to do; and the further management of affairs was left by the citizens to the committee of correspondence. On Monday, November 22d, 1773, the committees of Dorchester, Roxbury, Brookline, and Cambridge met the Boston Committee in the Selectmen's room in Faneuil Hall. At this conference of the five committees, it was unanimously voted to prevent the landing and sale of the tea, and to address a letter on the subject to all the towns in the province. On Sunday the 28th, the Dartmouth, the first of the tea ships, arrived. On the following day Samuel Adams invited the committees of Dorchester and the three other towns, to meet the committee and citizens of Boston in Faneuil Hall. This is the memorable meeting that was adjourned to the Old South church, at which it was resolved that the tea should be sent back to England. On the 30th, a meeting was held in Dorchester, at which it was resolved, that "should this country be so unhappy, as to see a day of trial for the recovery of its rights, by a last and solemn appeal to Him who gave them, we should not be behind the bravest of our patriotic brethren, and that we will at all times be ready to assist our neighbors and friends, when they shall need us, though in the greatest danger." (Rec. III., 407.) In the course of a few days, two more ships arrived; the committee of the six towns (for Charlestown had now been added) were in continual conference. The consignees were urged to send back the tea; the collector would not clear the vessels till the tea was discharged; the governor refused a permit to pass the castle, unless the ships were cleared. No peaceable solution of the problem remained, and on the night of the 16th December, a party of persons, disguised as Mohawk Indians, boarded the ships and threw into the water three hundred and forty-two chests of tea.

One of these chests, partly emptied, and buoyant, was borne by the tide to Dorchester neck, and there picked up on the morning of the 17th, by a person who saw it on the marshes and "thought it no harm." He was speedily required to surrender the article, and it was only after apology made in public town meeting, that he was forgiven for his indiscretion. (Rec. III., 414.)

The destruction of the tea, I need hardly say, occasioned the Boston port-bill, and the occupation of the town by a greatly increased military force. These measures on the part of the government were met by the organization of measures of resistance, military and political, on the part of the colonies. On the 24th of August, 1774, delegates were chosen by Dorchester, to attend the celebrated meeting at Dedham, of all the towns in the County of Suffolk, not as yet divided. A month later, instructions were given to Capt. Lemuel Robinson to represent the town in the general court to be held at Salem. The writs for the meeting having been recalled by General Gage, Capt. Robinson was authorized to meet the representatives of the other towns IN GENEral Provincial Congress, to "act upon such matters as might come before that body, in such a manner as may appear to him conducive to the true interest of this town and province, and most likely to preserve the liberties of all America." (Rec. III., 435.) The persons elected, to the number of ninety, assembled at Salem on the 5th of October, notwithstanding the recal of the writs. Having waited in vain for the appearance of the Governor to administer the usual oaths, they organized themselves into a convention the next day, with John Hancock as Chairman, and Benjamin Lincoln as Clerk. A committee was appointed to consider the proclamation of the Governor, and on their Report the following day (October 7th, 1774) it was voted, that "the members aforesaid do now resolve themselves into a Provincial Congress." This body adjourned the same day to Concord, and afterwards held its meetings at Watertown. Its formation followed, by one month, the meeting of the Continental Congress at Philadelphia, and it was, I believe, the first regularly organized body assembled in any of the States, and assuming legislative powers of a revolutionary character.

Among its acts was one which may be considered of itself as forming, as far as Massachusetts is concerned, a precise date to the revolution in the government, regarded as a political measure; I mean the recommendation to the towns to pay their quota of the Province tax not to the Receiver for the Crown, but to a treasurer appointed by this Provincial Congress. Dorchester, on the 27th Dec. 1774, complied with this recommendation, and resolved that "the collectors of this town pay the province tax, now in their hands or yet to be collected, to Henry Gardner, Esq., of Stow," a gentleman of sterling probity and a true patriot, prematurely removed from the stage of life; whose grandson, a native son of Dorchester, the chief magistrate of the Commonwealth, honors us with his presence on this occasion.

By another act equally decisive, the Provincial Congress of Massachusetts made military preparation for the approaching crisis. The enlistment of twenty thousand men was recommended, and officers of the seven years' war designated for the command.

In pursuance of this recommendation, Dorchester, on the 10th March, 1775, resolved that "the whole of the inhabitants of this town assemble on a certain day, those who are liable to do military duty with arms and ammunition *according to law*, in order to be reviewed, and to see whether any members of them will enlist and hold themselves in readiness as minute men; and those in the alarm list to choose officers to command them." (Rec. III., 442.)

On the 19th of April the all-important blow was struck; the blow which severed the fated chain whose every link was bolted by an act of Parliament, whose every rivet was closed up by an order in Council,—which bound to the wake of Europe the brave bark of our youthful fortune, destined henceforth and forever to ride the waves alone,—the blow which severed that fated chain was struck. The blow was struck, which will be felt in its consequences to ourselves and the family of nations, till the seventh seal is broken from the apocalyptic volume of the history of empires. The consummation of four centuries was completed. The life-long hopes and heart-sick visions of Columbus, poorly fulfilled in the subjugation of the plumed tribes of a few tropical islands, and the partial survey of the continent; cruelly mocked by the fetters placed upon his noble limbs by his own menial and which he carried with him into his grave, were at length more than fulfilled, when the new world of his discovery put on the sovereign robes of her separate national existence, and joined, for peace and for war, the great Panathenaic procession of the nations. The wrongs of generations were redressed. The cup of humiliation drained to the dregs by the old puritan confessors and non-conformist victims of oppression,—loathsome prisons, blasted fortunes, lips forbidden to open in prayer, earth and water denied in their pleasant native land, the separations and sorrows of exile, the sounding perils of the ocean, the scented hedge-rows and vocal thickets of the "old countrie" exchanged for a pathless wilderness ringing with the war-whoop and gleaming with the scalping-knife; the secular insolence of colonial rule, checked by no periodical recurrence to the public will; governors appointed on the other side of the globe that knew not Joseph; the patronizing disdain of undelegated power; the legal contumely of foreign law, wanting the first element of obligation, the consent of the governed expressed by his authorized representative; and at length the last unutterable and burning affront and shame, a mercenary soldiery encamped upon the fair eminences of our cities, ships of war with springs on their cables moored in front of our crowded quays, artillery planted open-mouthed in our principal streets, at the doors of our houses of assembly, their morning and evening salvos proclaiming to the rising and the setting sun, that we are the subjects and they the lords,—all these hideous phantoms of the long colonial night swept off by the first sharp volley on Lexington Green.

Well might Samuel Adams exclaim, as he heard it, "Oh, what a glorious morning is this!" glorious, but as is too often the case with human glories, the germ and the fruit of sorrow, sanctified with tears and sealed with blood. Precious lives are to be sacrificed, great trials public and private to be endured, seven years of war are to desolate the land, patriot armies are to march with bloody feet over ice-clad fields, a cloud of anxiety must hang over the prospects of one generation of the young, while another of the aged go down to the grave before the vision is fulfilled:—but still glorious at home and abroad,—glorious for America, and, strange as the word may sound, glorious even for England! Lord Chatham rejoiced that America had resisted. Surely Lord Chatham never rejoiced in the shame of England; he rejoiced that America had resisted, because she resisted on the great principles of constitutional liberty. Burke, in the early stages of the contest, wrote these golden words: "We view the establishment of the British Colonies on principles of liberty, as that which is to render this kingdom venerable to future ages. In comparison of this we regard all the victories and conquests of our warlike ancestors or of our own times as barbarous and vulgar distinctions, in which many nations whom we look upon with little respect or value, have equalled if not exceeded us. THIS IS THE PECULIAR GLORY OF ENGLAND!"* All the victories and conquests of our warlike ancestors or of our own times—Plantagenets and Tudors; Crecy, Poictiers, Agincourt; Dunkirk and Calais; Jamaica and Gibraltar; the Cromwells and the Blakes; the Williams and the Georges; the triumphs of Marlborough at the gates of France, the thunders of Clive on the banks of the Ganges; all, in Burke's judgment, barbarous distinctions, vulgar fame, compared with "the peculiar glory" of founding a colonial empire on the principles of liberty!

Of the great events which influenced the result of the revolution, few are more important than that which took place within our limits. At Lexington and Concord the great appeal to arms was irrevocably made. As the alarm of that day spread through the country, the men of Dorchester hastened to the field. They stood side by side with their countrymen, from every part of New England, when the great question of the capacity of a patriotic militia to contend with veteran troops was decided at Bunker Hill. But the occupation of our Heights produced a distinct strategic result, not inferior in importance to any other in the whole war. It was literally

* Burke's Works, Vol. II., 403.

*victoria sine clade ;* a noble victory achieved without the effusion of blood.

But there is another circumstance which must ever clothe the occupation of Dorchester Heights with an affecting interest. It was the first great military operation of Washington in the revolutionary war; not a battle, indeed, but the preparation for a battle on the grandest scale, planned with such skill and executed with such vigor, as at once to paralyze the army and navy of the enemy, and force him, without striking a blow, to an ignominious retreat. Washington was commissioned as Commander in Chief of the American Armies on the day the battle of Bunker Hill was fought. The siege of Boston had been already formed; and those noble lines of circumvallation, twelve miles in compass, of which some faint remains may still be traced, had been drawn along the high grounds of Charlestown, Cambridge, Roxbury, and Dorchester. An adventurous expedition against Quebec had failed; partial collisions had taken place wherever there were royal forces throughout the country; but nothing decisive was brought about, and a feverish excitement pervaded the continent. Congress was still conducting the war without a constitutional existence; and all eyes and hearts were turned to the army and to Washington. Men at a safe distance and with nothing at stake, are prone to judge severely the conduct of those who are at the post of responsibility and danger. Washington himself felt the delicacy and the hazards of his position; the importance of sustaining the expectations of the country; the necessity of decisive results. But his army was without discipline or experience, save a few veterans of the seven years' war, without adequate supplies of any kind, composed of men who had left their homes at a moment's warning and were impatient to return, weakened by camp diseases and the small-pox, with a stock of powder so scanty, that stratagem was resorted to by the commander to conceal the deficiency even from his officers. Thus the summer and the autumn wore away, and every week increased the public impatience and added to the embarrassments of Washington. His private letters at this time are filled with the most touching remarks on his distressed condition. In a letter to Colonel Reed, of the 14th of January, 1776, he says, "The reflection on my situation and that of this army, produces many an unhappy hour, when all around me are wrapped in sleep. Few people know the predicament we are in on a thousand accounts; fewer still will believe, if any disaster happens to these lines, from what cause it flows. I have often thought how much happier I should have been, if, instead of accepting the command under such circumstances, I had taken my musket on my shoulder and entered the ranks; or, if I could have justified the measure to posterity and my own conscience, had retired to the back country and lived in a wigwam."

At length, however, the re-enlistment of the army was completed; advanced lines were thrown up, ordnance captured at Ticonderoga had been transported by Knox with prodigious effort across the country, ammunition had been taken by Manly in his prize ships, shells were furnished from the royal arsenal at New York. It was Washington's wish to cross the ice to Boston, to carry the town by assault, and destroy the royal army. The ice, however, did not make till the middle of February; and it was decided, by a council of war, that the town could not be assaulted with success.

It was then resolved to repeat, on a grander scale, with full preparation and ample means, the hasty operation which had brought on the battle of Bunker Hill, the preceding summer. It was determined first to occupy the heights of Dorchester, and as soon as an impregnable position was secured there, to establish batteries on Nook Hill and the other rising grounds nearest Boston. The fleet in the harbor was within range of the heights; the town was commanded from the hills below. The occupation of these points would of necessity compel the enemy to take the risk of a decisive action, or to evacuate the town.

Washington, though preferring the bolder measure, yielded to the decision of his council, and threw his whole soul into the work. A plan for a grand combined movement was matured. The heights of Dorchester were to be occupied on the night of the 4th of March, in order that the anticipated battle might be fought on the anniversary of the ever-memorable 5th of March, 1770. As soon as the conflict was engaged on the heights, Putnam was to cross from Cambridge with a body of four thousand men, land in two divisions in Boston, and forcing his way through the town burst open the fortifications on the neck, and thus admit a division of the American army from Roxbury. To distract and occupy the attention of the enemy, the town was severely bombarded from Somerville, East Cambridge and Roxbury, during the nights of the 2d, 3d, and 4th of March.

I am told by professional men that these dispositions evince consummate military skill; and are among the facts which show that Washington, too often compelled by his situation to pursue the Fabian policy, possessed a talent for military combinations that entitles him to a place beside the greatest captains of the last century.

The 4th of March, the day so long and anxiously expected, at length arrives. The troops are put in motion in the evening, from the American lines at Roxbury and Dorchester. An advanced guard of eight hundred men precedes; the carts with intrenching tools came next, with the main body, twelve hundred strong, under General Thomas; the whole followed by a train of three hundred wagons loaded with fascines, gabions, and bundles of hay. They crossed Dorchester neck without being perceived, and reached their destination in two divisions, one for each of the heights. Bundles of hay were placed on the side of the causeway, at the most exposed parts, as a protection in case the enemy should discover and attempt to interrupt the movement. Under this shelter, parties from the American army passed several times during the night, without being perceived, though it was bright moonlight. This was owing, no doubt, to the cannonade and bombardment of the town from the opposite quarter, by which also the whole surrounding country was thrown into a state of painful expectation and alarm. The operations were conducted by Gridley, an experienced engineer of the old French war. He was aided by Col. Putnam, in laying out and executing the works, which before morning, though incomplete, were adequate against grape-shot and musketry.

Washington was present on the heights. In the strictness of military duty, the presence of the commander-in-chief of the army was not required on the ground, on such an occasion; but the operation was too important to be trusted entirely to subordinates. Accompanied by Mr. James Bowdoin, then a young man of twenty-two, afterwards your respected fellow citizen, and the representative of Dorchester in the Convention of Massachusetts which adopted the Constitution of the United States, Washington, whose head quarters were at Cambridge, repaired, on this eventful night, to Dorchester heights.* He has left no record descriptive of the scene, or of his thoughts and emotions at what he must have regarded, at that time, as the most eventful hour of his life, and the most critical moment of the war. "The moon shining in its full lustre" (they are the words of Washington), revealed every object through the clear cold air of early March, with that spectral distinctness, with

* Eulogy on Hon. James Bowdoin, by Rev. Dr. Jenks, p. 19, 20; Addresses and Speeches, by Hon. R. C. Winthrop, p. 109.

which things present themselves to the straining eye, at a great juncture. All immediately around him intense movement, but carried on in death-like silence; nothing heard but the incessant tread of busy feet, and the dull sound of the mattock upon the soil, frozen so deep as to make it necessary to place the chief reliance on the fascines and gabions. Beneath him, the slumbering batteries of the castle; the roadstead and harbor filled with the vessels of the royal fleet, motionless except as they swung round at their moorings at the turn of the midnight tide; the beleaguered city, occupied by a powerful army and a considerable non-combatant population, startled into unnatural vigilance by the incessant and destructive cannonade, but yet unobservant of the great operations in progress so near them; the surrounding country, dotted with a hundred rural settlements, roused from the deep sleep of a New England village by the unwonted tumult and glare.

It has been stated, in one or two well-authenticated cases of persons restored after drowning, where life has been temporarily extinguished in the full glow of health, with the faculties unimpaired by disease and in perfect action, that, in the last few minutes of conscious existence, the whole series of the events of the entire life comes rushing back to the mind, distinctly but with inconceivable rapidity; that the whole life is lived over again in a moment. Such a narrative, by a person of high official position in a foreign country, and perfect credibility, I have read. We may well suppose that at this most critical moment of Washington's life, a similar concentration of thought would take place, and that the events of his past existence as they had prepared him for it,—his training while yet a boy in the wilderness, his escape from drowning and the rifle of the savage on his perilous mission to Venango, the shower of iron hail through which he rode unharmed on Braddock's field, would now crowd through his memory; that much more also the past life of his country, the early stages of the great conflict now brought to its crisis, and still more solemnly the possibilities of the future for himself and for America, would press upon him; the ruin of the patriotic cause if he failed at the outset; the triumphant consolidation of the revolution if he prevailed; with higher visions of the hopeful family of rising States, their auspicious growth and prosperous fortunes, hovering like a dream of angels in the remoter prospect;—all this, attended with the immense desire of honest fame (for we cannot think even Washington's mind too noble to possess the "last infirmity"), the intense inward glow of manly heroism about to act its great part on a sublime theatre,—the softness of the man chastening the severity of the chieftain, and deeply touched at the sufferings and bereavements about to be caused by the conflict of the morrow; the still tenderer emotions that breathed their sanctity over all the rest; the thought of the faithful and beloved wife who had followed him from Mount Vernon, and of the aged mother whose heart was aching in her Virginia home for glad tidings of "George, who was always a good boy,"—all these pictures, visions, feelings, pangs;—too vast for words, too deep for tears,—but swelling, no doubt, in one unuttered prayer to Heaven, we may well imagine to have filled the soul of Washington at that decisive hour, as he stood upon the heights of Dorchester, with the holy stars for his camp-fire, and the deep folding shadows of night, looped by the hand of God to the four quarters of the sky, for the curtains of his tent.*

The morning of the 5th of March dawned, and the enemy beheld with astonishment, looming through a heavy mist, the operations of the night. Gen. Howe wrote to the minister that they must have been the work of at least twelve thousand men. In the account given by one of his officers, and adopted in the Annual Register, it is said that the expedition with which these works were thrown up, with their sudden and unexpected appearance, "recalled to the mind those wonderful stories of enchantment

---

* This imagery was partly suggested to me by a noble stanza in Gleim's Ode on the victory gained by Frederic the Great, at Lowositz, dimly retained in a recollection of forty years. Since the Address was delivered, my friend, Prof. Felton, has at my request, with the kind aid of Dr. Beck, helped me to the original, which is as follows:—

"Auf einer Trommel sass der Held,
Und dachte seine Schlacht;
Den Himmel über sich zum Zelt,
Und um sich her die Nacht."

Nearly in English as follows:—

Upon a drum the hero sat,
And thought upon his fight;
The heaven above him for his tent,
And all around the night.

and invisible agency, which are so frequent in the Eastern romances."

General Howe, like a gallant commander, immediately determined on the perilous attempt to dislodge the Americans before their entrenchments should be rendered impregnable. A powerful detachment, led by Lord Percy, dropped down to the castle in the afternoon, to rendezvous there, and thence cross over to Dorchester point, and storm the heights. A heavy gale (a "dreadful storm," it is called, in the British account) scattered the barges, and prevented the embarkation of the troops. This delay gave the Americans time to perfect their works, barrels filled with earth were placed round the heights, an *abattis* of trees disposed around the foot of the hill, a reinforcement of two thousand men ordered to the support of General Thomas, and every preparation made for a decisive conflict.*

It was soon understood that the royal commander, not deeming it safe to take the risk of an engagement, had determined to evacuate Boston. To prevent the destruction of the town, Washington was willing that they should leave it unmolested. Finding, however, after some days, that no apparent movement was made for this purpose, he determined without further delay to occupy Nook hill and the other elevations fronting and commanding the town. This produced the desired effect, and General Howe was at length compelled to acknowledge the inability of a powerful land and naval force, under veteran

---

* Heath's Memoirs, p. 40.

leaders, to maintain themselves against untried levies whom they were accustomed to regard with contempt, led by officers from whom they affected even to withhold the usual titles of military command. He was obliged to acquiesce in an engagement with the Selectmen of Boston, tacitly sanctioned by "Mr. Washington," that his army should be allowed to embark without being fired upon, on condition that they would not burn the town.*

Thus, on the 17th of March, 1776, an effective force of many thousand men evacuated the town, and with a powerful fleet and a numerous train of transports, sailed for Halifax. Putnam, with a detachment of the American army, took possession of Boston. The beloved commander himself made his entry into the town the following day, and the first great act of the drama of the Revolution was brought to a triumphant close, on that old Dorchester Neck which, before the foundation of Boston, our fathers selected as a place for settlement.

This event diffused joy throughout the Union, and contributed materially to prepare the public mind for that momentous political measure, of which we this day commemorate the seventy-ninth anniversary. That civil government, however human infirmities mingle in its organization, is, in its ultimate principles, a Divine ordinance, will be doubted by no one who believes in an overruling Providence. That every people has a right to interpret for itself the will of Providence, in reference to the form of gov-

---

* Newell's Journal, Mass. Hist. Collections, Fourth Series, Vol. I., 272.

ernment best suited to its condition, subject to no external human responsibility, is equally certain, and is the doctrine which lies at the basis of the Declaration of Independence. But what makes a People,—what constitutes this august community, to which we give that name; how many persons—how few; bound to each other by what antecedent ties of physical descent, of common language, of local proximity, of previous political connection? This is a great question, to which no answer, that I know, has yet been given; to which, in general terms, perhaps, none can be given. Physiologists have not yet found the seat of animal life,—far less of the rational intellect or spiritual essence of the individual Man. Who can wonder that it should be still farther beyond our ability to define the mysterious laws which,—out of the physical instincts of our nature, the inexplicable attractions of kindred and tongue, the persuasions of reason, the social sympathies, the accidents as we call them of birth, the wanderings of nations in the dark ages of the past, the confederacies of peace, the ravages of war, employed by the all-fashioning hand of time, which moulds every thing human according to the eternal types in the divine mind,—work out, in the lapse of centuries, with more than Promethean skill, that wondrous creation which we call A PEOPLE!

The Declaration of Independence which we celebrate to-day, attempted no definition of these mysterious agencies; it assumed their result. It assumed that the late Colonies of England were a People, and entitled to all the rights implied in the name.

"When, in the course of human events, it becomes necessary for one People to dissolve the political bands which have connected them with another, and to assume among the powers of the earth the separate and equal station to which the laws of nature and nature's God entitle them, a decent respect for the opinions of mankind requires that they should declare the causes that impel them to the separation." Such is the dignified and solemn commencement of the great instrument by which, seventy-nine years ago, with the hearty concurrence of the citizens of Dorchester, the Continental Congress of America, renouncing allegiance to the British government, asserted the Independence of these United States.* They left,—they were com-

---

* The Council of Massachusetts directed (July 17th, 1776) that a copy of the Declaration should be sent to each minister of every denomination in the State, to be read to his congregation, and then handed to the town clerks, "who are required to record the same in their respective town or district books, there to remain as a perpetual memorial thereof." It is found in Dorchester Records III., p. 461—5.

It is a matter of interest to compare the Declaration of the Independence of the United States of America, of the 4th July, 1776, with that of the States General of the United Provinces of Holland, of the 26th of July, 1581, by which they asserted their independence of the Spanish Crown. The two Declarations are necessarily altogether different in their details, but as the occasions which produced them are alike, so there is a similarity in their structure, and in the mode of treating the subject, which I hardly think can be mere coincidence. I have a black letter copy of the original in Dutch, printed at Leyden by the sworn Printer of the State of Holland, in 1581, with this title:—Placcaet vande Staten generael vande ghevnieerde Nederlanden: byden welcken, midts den redenen in't lange in't selfde begrepen, men verclaert den Coninck van Spaegnien vervallen vande Ouerheyt ende Heerschappije van dese voors. Nederlanden, ende verbiet sijnen naem ende zeghel inde selue Landen meer te ghebruycken, &c. A translation is contained in Lord Somers's Tracts, Vol. I., p. 323, Sir Walter Scott's Edition.

pelled to leave it to the bloody arbitrament of war, whether they were rebellious colonies to be lawfully reduced by force, or a sovereign people rightfully struggling to be free.

Happy for humanity would it be, if this question could find a peaceful and practical solution. It will, in the coming centuries, perhaps in times near at hand, be a frequently recurring question. Vast colonial dependencies exist in various parts of the world, subject to the powers of Western Europe. Such is the case with half the continent of North America; with all the West India Islands, with a single exception; with an immense region of southern Africa; with the vast territory of India, and with most of the islands of the Indian Archipelago; and with the whole Australian world. There is no reason to doubt that, in the lapse of time, these colonial dependencies will grow up in population, in wealth, in intelligence, and in all the elements of political life, to the stature of a perfect State. How devoutly is it to be wished that principles of public law should be established, regulating the transition of colonies into a condition of Independence, by great constitutional compacts, and not through the gates of bloody revolution!

There is another momentous question which is left undecided in the great declaration; and that is, whether all the inhabitants of British America in their united capacity, and in that alone, formed the "one People" which asserted their independence (which was perhaps the opinion generally entertained by the statesmen of 1776), or whether the inhabitants of the several colonies were each a people who, if it had pleased them, could each have declared its separate independence (as some appear afterwards to have held and to hold);—this was a question not discussed this day seventy-nine years ago. That was a period of high patriotic excitement, of fervid sentiment, of impulsive effort against an impending danger. The metaphysics of state are an afterthought of prosperous and speculative times. But, however these questions may be decided, whatever foundation there may be for the opinion that the inhabitants of each State in the Union are entitled to the name and rights of an independent people; it may be safely affirmed that they cannot at one and the same time be the people of two different States or Territories; although the contrary doctrine seems to prevail to some extent, I trust not widely, in the West, where it has lately been maintained, by the sharp logic of the revolver and the Bowie-knife, that the people of Missouri are the people of Kanzas!

It would have been a pleasing task, fellow citizens, had time permitted it, to pursue this rapid glance at the fortunes of our native town, through the period which has elapsed from the Declaration of Independence to the present time. Such a glance would have exhibited, at least since the commencement of this century, a picture of steady growth and almost uninterrupted prosperity, of which few brighter examples can be found in the Commonwealth. It is within this period that my own family associations with Dorchester, and my personal recollections, fall. I seem even now to hear the voice of the same ancient bell which cheered us this morning with its festal peal, as fifty-five years ago it called together the citizens of Dorchester to the meeting-house on yonder hill, to listen to the eulogy on Washington from the lips of one, whom I was called too soon to deplore; and who is not to be named by me, after the lapse of so many years, but with tenderness and veneration.* In this period, under the influence of the principles of solid national growth which gave character to the earliest settlements of Massachusetts, and of which, thank heaven, the force is not yet expended, of that love of liberty which prompted the Declaration of Independence, and of that spirit of fraternal affection which produced the last great fruit of the revolution, —the union of the States under a constitution of confederated republican government,—our country has increased in population, in wealth, in strength, in all that benefits or adorns the societies of men, till it stands the admiration of the world. O fortunatos nimium, sua si bona norint! Happy, too happy, did we but know our blessings. Perfection belongs to nothing human. Times of trial have come upon the country, at different periods; wars abroad and dissensions at home,—alarming junctures of affairs;—and these vicissitudes must be anticipated in time to come as they have happened in time past. But hitherto an unfailing good Providence has carried us through the trials, without which this world would come too near perfection. Let us, my

---

* A eulogy on Washington was, at the request of the citizens of Dorchester, delivered on the 22d February, 1800, by my honored father, Oliver Everett, who died 19th December, 1802.

fellow citizens, on this anniversary of the nation's birth, rescue one day from the cruel dominion of those passions which fill us with bitterness toward each other, and unite in the hope, that we shall still be sustained by the same Almighty arm which bore our fathers over the waters,—supported them under the hardships of the first settlement,—conducted them through the difficulties of the colonial period, —protected them through the dangers of the revolutionary struggle,—and has guided their career as an independent State.

Thus, my friends, in the neighborhood of the spot where, in my early childhood, I acquired the first elements of learning at one of those public schools, which are the glory and strength of New England, I have spoken to you imperfectly of the appropriate topics of the day. Retired from public life, without the expectation or the wish to return to it, but the contrary,—grateful for the numerous marks of public confidence which I have received, and which I feel to be beyond my merits,—respecting the convictions of those from whom I have at any time differed, and asking the same justice for my own,—I confess, fellow citizens, that few things would better please me than to find a quiet retreat in my native town, where I might pass the rest of my humble career in the serious studies and tranquil pursuits which befit the decline of life, till the same old bell should announce that the chequered scene is over, and the weary is at rest.

AN ACCOUNT OF THE

# CELEBRATION IN DORCHESTER,

## JULY 4, 1855.

---

THE SEVENTY-NINTH ANNIVERSARY

OF

## AMERICAN INDEPENDENCE,

AND THE

**TWO HUNDRED AND TWENTY-FIFTH YEAR**

FROM THE

## LANDING OF THE FIRST SETTLERS.

# PRELIMINARY PROCEEDINGS.

---

In the year 1853, a letter, numerously signed by citizens of Dorchester, was addressed to the Hon. Edward Everett, inviting him to deliver an oration in honor of the Declaration of Independence. Upon Mr. Everett's acceptance of the invitation, in the succeeding year, a meeting of the citizens of Dorchester was convened, and a large committee appointed with full authority to make all necessary arrangements for the proper observance of the day, and also to commemorate the two hundred and twenty-fifth anniversary of the settlement of the town.

---

## CORRESPONDENCE.

### LETTER TO MR. EVERETT FROM THE CITIZENS OF DORCHESTER.

Hon. EDWARD EVERETT. *Dorchester, October* 10, 1853.

Sir:

Actuated by motives of public good, and believing in the salutary teachings of national events when contemplated with an inquiring spirit and enlightened judgment —the undersigned, citizens of Dorchester, without distinction of party, are desirous of celebrating the 4th of July,

1854, in a manner that shall prove creditable to that ancient town, instructive to the young, renovating to the aged, and morally profitable to the nation.

Although the occasion is one of annual occurrence, its magnitude increases with every revolution of the great wheel of progress, and the growing and diversified interests of the country are unceasingly presenting new and momentous questions to be studied, illustrated and explained. The asylum of freedom, and equally the director of progress, America, in her youth, stands in the highly responsible positions of both protector and pioneer; and while it is her ambition to secure an unquestionable efficiency in the one, it is no less her pride to aim at the highest standard of wisdom in the other.

Placed in such fearful relations of responsibility, and held strictly accountable to posterity for the faithfulness with which they perform the sacred duties of citizenship, the American people owe it to the achievements of the past, to the bloody toils and sacrifices of their ancestors; to their hopes and aspirations as immortal beings for the advancement of their descendants, and to the universal cause of humanity in the immeasurable future,—so to sanctify and ennoble the great birth-day of freedom by constantly associating with it the cheering and weighty events of progress, as to render identical the power of knowledge and the blessings of freedom. The intellect should be trained to acknowledge and to practise the true means of happiness. Such a theme demands a patriot's spirit, a statesman's knowledge, and a master's skill. It is a lesson to be taught to an entire nation,—to the observers of all nations. It is a subject narrowed to no limits of Township, Commonwealth, or Country, but illimitable as the workings in the invisible and unfathomable depths and recesses of the soul.

The humble but ancient town of Dorchester, though once

the chief of New England, affords but a slender stock of materials for the scrutinizing historian. Still, its annals are not entirely void of national interest. Its early example of Town organization, and the zeal of her sons to extend the domain of truth, and to give form to the colonizing spirit in distant sections of the continent, were characteristic indications of its first settlers. Its Heights were made to frown upon an invading foe, and its brave citizens were among the first to resist the acts of British oppression. Its hills were honored by a Bowdoin, and its plains by a Stoughton and an Everett.

In asking you to address the people of Dorchester, and such others as may honor the occasion with their presence, on the 4th of July 1854, the subscribers are not unmindful of your important and laborious position in the councils of the nation, and of those numerous engagements ever incident to the transcendant gifts and acquirements of mind. It is hoped, however, that the place of your nativity may be regarded in the present case with an indulgent and special consideration,—believing, as we do, that whatever and whenever you speak as a statesman, the people of a nation will seek to become acquainted with your counsels.

We have the honor to be, with considerations of respect and esteem, your most obedient servants and fellow citizens.

Oliver Hall,
Ebenezer Eaton,
Samuel P. Loud,
John Kettell,
Edward King,
Daniel Denny,
David Cummins,
Charles Hood,
Marshall P. Wilder,
Edward Sharp,
John G. Nazro,
Thomas Groom,
M. Field Fowler,
Thomas Tremlett,
Nathaniel R. Childs,
Nathan Carruth,
Henry Gardner,
John Barnard,
Wm. Worthington,
Charles Ranstead,
M. O. Barry,
Wm. P. Barnard,
A. C. Dorr,
Wm. H. Richardson,
John H. Sumner,
Samuel Gilbert, Jr.

Lorenzo Prouty,
Thomas M. Vinson,
Elisha Preston,
E. P. Tileston,
Willam D. Swan,
Thomas D. Quincy,
Lewis Pierce,
Eleazer J. Bispham,
Darius Brewer,
J. B. Robb,
John H. Robinson,
Ebenezer Clapp,
George Richardson,
John Richardson,
Cornelius Bird,
William Richardson,
Nahum Capen,
Edward Everett Rice,
James Tucker, Jr.
Nath'l E. Tucker,
Wm. E. Vincent,
James Sivret,
Henry J. Gardner,
Eben. Clapp, Jr.
Seth C. Jones,
C. M. Thompson,
E. P. Robinson,
Harvey Howe,
W. A. Gilbert,
Charles Hunt,
Amos Upham,
Charles Bradlee,
Robert Richardson,
Samuel J. Capen,
Joseph Tuttle,
Thomas M. Mosely,
Nath'l W. Tileston,
John C. Brown,
Charles B. Peirce,
Charles Howe,
Elijah Vose,
James Jenkins,
William Clap,
T. J. Vinton,
James Swan,
William Pope, Jr.
J. P. Clapp,
Charles Emery,
Williams B. Brooks,
Charles H. Pierce,
O. Putnam Bacon,
Otis Wright,
Wm. H. Chamberlain,
Charles Lane,
J. W. Pottle,
Wm. F. Worthington,
Elisha H. Preston,
John Preston, 2d,
Richard Pitts,
O. A. Farwell,
George M. Browne,
John W. Blanchard,
Edmund Wright,
Wm. E. Abbot,
Robert Pierce,
S. B. Pierce,
Robert Vose,
Samuel E. Sawyer,
James W. Sever,
Charles P. Ripley,
Roswell Gleason,
George Haynes,
R. F. Tolman,
Nath'l F. Safford,
Amasa Pray,
Ebenezer Holden,
Robert Codman,
William Tolman,
Benjamin Cushing,
Benjamin Jacobs,
John W. Porter,
Robert Rhodes,
Nathan Holbrook,
John P. Spooner,
Eben Tolman,
George C. Thacher,
John J. May,
D. E. Wadleigh,
Daniel Lane,
John Mears,
Barnabas Davis,
Thomas Howe,
Samuel B. Pierce, 2d,
Isaac Clapp,

Edward Jarvis,
Charles Ansorge,
T. H. Cleveland,
Wm. R. Austin,
Augustus Brown,
William T Andrews,
Oliver Downing,
James H. Upham,
Enoch Train,
Samuel Swan,
Dean F. Battles,
Bradish Billings,
John O. B. Minot,
Fred. F. Hassam,
Samuel Hall,
E. H. R. Ruggles,
John Burt,
Edmund J. Baker,
W. F. Temple,
H. Temple,
Cheever Newhall,
Edward Jones,
Wm. M. Jackson,
Frederick Nichols,
John Fox,
G. W. Boynton,
Thomas C. Wales,
Nath'l Hall,
Henry Lunt,
George W. Porter,
George Yendell,
S. S. Curtis,
J. H. Pray,
John A. Pray,
Wm. H. Pray.

---

LETTER OF COMMITTEE OF INVITATION.

*Dorchester, October* 10, 1853.

Hon. EDWARD EVERETT,

Sir:

We have the honor to present to you a communication, numerously signed by citizens of Dorchester, and respectfully ask that you will give to the subject of it the most favorable consideration consistent with your convictions of duty.

The Committee, in performing the agreeable duty assigned to them, take great pleasure in extending to you the assurance, that could the celebration take place as proposed in the communication now presented, it has the promise of being singularly distinguished by the spirit of unanimity and of patriotism.

With high considerations of respect and true regard, we have the honor to be your most obedient servants,

Marshall P. Wilder,
Daniel Denny,
William T. Andrews,
Nahum Capen,
Robert Codman,
*Com. of Invitation.*

MR. EVERETT'S REPLY.

*Boston, November* 30, 1854.

GENTLEMEN :—

You are aware, through my personal communications with Mr. Capen, of the reasons which prevented me, a twelvemonth since, from returning a formal answer to the invitation of a very large number of the citizens of Dorchester, transmitted to me with your letter of the 10th of October, 1853, to deliver an oration on the 4th of July of the present year.

My Congressional duties at that time forbade my entering into an engagement for the 4th of July last, and you were pleased to propose the extension of the invitation to the 4th of July, 1855.

I cannot but feel gratified and honored by an invitation proceeding from so large a number of the most respected citizens of the town where I was born and passed my childhood, and at whose schools I received the rudiments of my education. I have been obliged for many years, in consequence of the very great number of applications to address public meetings of every kind, to excuse myself almost altogether; and I might find, in the state of my health and other domestic circumstances, an apology for declining this invitation. But I cannot resist the temptation to avail myself of this opportunity, to address my fellow citizens of Dorchester, for the first time in my life, and to unite with them in a festival, which, as I infer from the communication with which you have favored me, has been projected with more than usual thoughtful reference to the nature and consequences of the great event commemorated.

With these feelings, gentlemen, I accept with pleasure the invitation which I have received through you from a large number of the citizens of Dorchester, without distinction of party, to deliver an oration before them on the fourth of July next.

I remain, with great respect, gentlemen, sincerely yours,

EDWARD EVERETT.

HON. MARSHALL P. WILDER,
DANIEL DENNY, ESQ.
WILLIAM T. ANDREWS, ESQ.
NAHUM CAPEN, ESQ.
ROBERT CODMAN, ESQ.

# OFFICERS AND COMMITTEES.

---

PRESIDENT OF THE DAY.

## MARSHALL P. WILDER.

VICE PRESIDENTS.

Samuel P. Loud,
Ebenezer Clapp,
William Clapp,
William Pope,
Henry Lunt,
Samuel B. Pierce, Sen.,
John Barnard,
Lewis Pierce,
Ebenezer Eaton,
Daniel Denny,
Thomas J. Tolman,
J. P. Spooner,
Isaac Clapp,
John Preston,
Enoch Train,
Edmund P. Tileston,
Charles Hood,
Edward King,
Roswell Gleason,
Cheever Newhall,
Oliver Hall,
E. J. Baker,
William D. Swan,
James Tolman,
Timothy Farrer,
Nathaniel Crane,
Edward Capen,
John Mears,
William E. Vincent,
John H. Robinson,
William T. Andrews,
E. J. Bispham,
Robert Vose,
E. H. R. Ruggles,
Charles Hunt,
Asaph Churchill,
Samuel B. Pierce, 2d,
Thomas Groom,
Wm. Richardson, *River st.*
Charles Howe,
John J. May,
Richard Baker, Jr.,
Thomas C. Wales,
Nathaniel F. Safford,
Thomas Liversidge,
Edmund Wright,
Samuel Gilbert, Jr.,
G. M. Browne,
William E. Abbot,
Dana Tucker,
Thomas Kendrick.

EXECUTIVE COMMITTEE.

Marshall P. Wilder,
Edmund P. Tileston,
Daniel Denny,
William D. Swan,
Oliver Hall,
John H. Robinson,
Aaron D. Capen,
Edward King,
Nahum Capen,
Enoch Train,
Nathan Carruth,
E. J. Bispham,
Charles Hunt,
Lewis Pierce.

Nahum Capen, *Secretary.*
Oliver Hall, *Treasurer.*

COMMITTEE ON INVITATIONS.

| | | |
|---|---|---|
| Samuel P. Loud, | Edmund J. Baker, | John P. Spooner, |
| Nahum Capen, | Ebenezer Clapp, Jr., | Robert Codman, |
| | W. E. Abbot. | |

COMMITTEE ON FINANCE.

| | | |
|---|---|---|
| Daniel Denny, | Thomas Howe, | William T. Andrews, |
| Enoch Train, | James Tucker, Jr., | Charles Lane, |
| Samuel Hall, | Cheever Newhall, | Oliver Hall. |

COMMITTEE ON RECEPTION.

| | | |
|---|---|---|
| Edmund P. Tileston, | Charles Howe, | William Codman, |
| Erastus D. Miller, | John J. May, | William H. Vincent. |
| Benj. Cushing, | Samuel J. Capen, | |

COMMITTEE ON SENTIMENTS AND SPEECHES.

| | | |
|---|---|---|
| William T. Andrews, | Asaph Churchill, | Edward Jarvis, |
| N. F. Safford, | Charles Hood, | E. J. Baker, |
| | William D. Swan. | |

COMMITTEE ON MUSIC.

| | | |
|---|---|---|
| Nathan Carruth, | James Jenkins, | James Swan, |
| Charles Bradlee, | William P. Barnard, | O. P. Bacon. |
| Samuel Gilbert, Jr., | Edward Everett Rice, | |

COMMITTEE ON MILITARY.

| | | |
|---|---|---|
| Col. J. W. Sever, | Capt. Harvey Howe, | Capt. Amasa Pray, |
| Maj. Aaron D. Capen, | Capt. Roswell Gleason, | Maj. M. G. Cobb. |

COMMITTEE ON PLACE OF MEETING AND ORDER OF PROCESSION.

| | | |
|---|---|---|
| Oliver Hall, | Robert Vose, | John Mears, Jr., |
| Lewis Pierce, | Edward Jones, | Ebenezer Eaton. |
| James Tolman, | E. J. Bispham, | |

COMMITTEE ON DINNER AND DECORATIONS.

| | | |
|---|---|---|
| John H. Robinson, | John Mears, | George Haynes, |
| Samuel B. Pierce, 2d, | William Pope, Jr., | Parker Barnes, |
| Joseph Tuttle, | Thomas Groom, | Thomas Kendrick, |
| Otis Wright, | George Yendell, | William Wales. |

COMMITTEE ON FIREWORKS.

| | | |
|---|---|---|
| Edward King, | Benjamin Jacobs, | A. W. Spencer, |
| John Preston, 2d, | J. H. Upham, | F. S. Drake, |
| M. O. Barry, | Fred. F. Hassam, | Robert Vose, Jr. |
| Wm. H. Richardson, | George H. Vincent, | |

CHIEF MARSHAL.

MOSES G. COBB.

AIDS.

| | | |
|---|---|---|
| C. C. Holbrook, | George F. Pierce, | C. M. Thompson, |
| Frank Tileston, | Thomas W. Tuttle, | A. W. Spencer. |

ASSISTANT MARSHALS.

| | | |
|---|---|---|
| George H. Vincent, | N. W. Coffin, | Augustus Parker, |
| E. W. Howe, | M. L. Bradford, | G. H. Kingsbury, |
| Geo. Woodman, | A. Donaldson, | Frank Pierce, |
| A. L. Jordan, | R. Gleason, Jr., | S. B. Mandell, |
| Charles F. Preston, | Samuel J. Capen, | E. W. Lincoln, |
| Charles H. Pierce, | William P. Leavitt, | Joseph D. Robinson, |
| Harvey Howe, | Sylvester H. Hebard, | Barney Ford, Jr., |
| Benjamin Cushing, | Thomas M. Vinson, | J. W. Porter, |
| A. D. Swan, | George Fisher, | J. B. Callender, |
| F. F. Hassam, | Robert White, | Wm. W. Swan, |
| F. S. Drake, | Jno. C. Robinson, | George W. Mears, |
| Robert Vose, Jr., | Alfred Clapp, | Gideon Beck, |
| Henry G. Denny, | Eben Bird, | Robert Cunningham, |
| J. Henry Loud, | Laban Pratt, | W. J. Robie, |
| Wm. H. Wilder, | Amasa Pray, | B. F. Brown, |
| George Newhall, | Eben. Holden, Jr., | F. B. Snow, |
| Anson Hardy, | C. A. Clapp, | Isaac Swan, |
| Axel Dearborn, | W. W. Paige, | E. G. Emery. |

# CEREMONIES OF THE DAY.

---

The morning proved to be one of the most delightful and balmy of the season, not a cloud obscuring the sky. During the day no accident occurred to mar its festivities; and throughout the various ceremonies of the occasion, there was but one expression of feeling—that of the highest enjoyment and satisfaction.

At sunrise, noon and sunset, salutes of cannon were fired from Mount Bowdoin and Commercial Point, by the Boston Light Artillery. The bells of the various Churches were rung, and other customary patriotic ceremonials of the day observed. Our national banner was thrown to the breeze from a hundred different flag-staffs, and as it floated over and among the delightful groves, looked more beautiful than ever. The magnificent staff erected on Meeting-House Hill, and the immense flag which floated from its top—both of which were furnished for the occasion through the liberality of Col. Enoch Train—attracted universal attention and admiration.

At an early hour, throngs of people from various quarters began to repair to the good old town of Dorchester, where they were cordially and hospitably received by the inhabitants, who were well prepared to greet their visitors. The public conveyances, cars and omnibuses, carried full loads, while the roads were filled with private carriages. Many houses in the principal streets were handsomely decorated, and before the hour for commencing the more public proceedings of the day, the visitors from abroad were numbered by thousands.

The invited guests assembled, at 9 o'clock, at the beautiful residence of William T. Andrews, Esq. The procession, which was large and imposing, was formed in Pleasant street, under the direction of Major Moses G. Cobb, Chief Marshal; the following gentlemen acting as aids:—C. C. Holbrook, Frank Tileston, George F. Pierce, Thomas W. Tuttle, C. M. Thompson, and A. W. Spencer.

The procession was preceded by a cavalcade, which presented, under the command of Lieut. Axel Dearborn, a fine appearance.

The escort duty was, by particular invitation, performed by the Independent Corps of Cadets, of Boston, under the command of Lieutenant Colonel Thomas C. Amory. They turned out sixty guns, and constituted a brilliant feature of the procession. The Weymouth Brass Band furnished the music.

The following was the order of the

## PROCESSION.

Cavalcade.

Independent Company of Cadets.

Committee of Arrangements.

Vice Presidents.

(IN CARRIAGES,)

The President of the Day and the Orator.

The Reader of the Declaration of Independence and the Chaplains.

His Excellency the Governor and Staff.

United States Senators and Representatives.

Lieut. Governor and Executive Council.
Officers of the Massachusetts Legislature.
President and Ex-Presidents of Harvard University.
Judges of the Courts in the State.
Officers of the War of 1812.
United States Officers, civil and military.
Descendants of Dorchester resident elsewhere.
Clergy and distinguished guests.

Next came a boat on wheels, called the "Everett Barge." It was filled with a delegation of fifteen children from the Everett School, all handsomely attired.

FIRE DEPARTMENT.

The several companies formed on Adams street, at 9 o'clock, A.M., accompanied by the Boston Brigade and Stoughton Brass Bands, and marched through Centre, Washington, Bowdoin and Commercial streets to Pleasant street, where they took their position in the procession, in the following order:—

SYLVESTER H. HEBARD, Chief Engineer.

Alfred Clapp, Robert White, Joseph C. Robinson and George L. Fisher, Assistant Engineers.

| | | | | |
|---|---|---|---|---|
| Fountain | Company, | No. 1, | George S. Esty, | Foreman. |
| Protector | " | No. 2, | Samuel F. White, | " |
| Torrent | " | No. 3, | Seth D. Durell, | " |
| Alert | " | No. 4, | Joseph W. Sloan, | " |
| Independence | " | No. 5, | Andrew Collins, | " |
| Tiger | " | No. 6, | James H. Upham, | " |

These companies turned out with full ranks, in new and appropriate uniform. The engines were beautifully decorated, and each one was drawn by two or four horses.

This Department, with their banners and decorations, added greatly to the interesting pageant.

A deputation of thirty-one members of the Order of United Americans, dressed in continental uniform, were represented in the procession. They appeared in a barge, which was drawn by eight splendid gray horses. Then followed the

Dorchester Antiquarian and Historical Society.

Town Officers of Dorchester.

School Committee.

Representatives to the General Court.

Subscribers to the Dinner.

CITIZENS.

The procession moved at 10 minutes past eleven, and took up Mr. EVERETT at the house in which he was born, at the corner of Pond and Boston streets. It then passed through Pond, Boston, Hancock, Bowdoin and Webster streets, to the Pavilion, where the Oration was delivered.

As the procession passed through Webster street, the scene was beautiful beyond description. The public schools had been formed in a line on either side of the street, with distinctive and appropriate banners. The boys were dressed in white pants and dark jackets, and the girls in white, their hats and bonnets being tastefully trimmed with wreaths and flowers. The various schools were distinguished by gay rosettes and sashes of different colors, and the children carried beautiful bouquets of flowers, which were scattered with liberal profuseness; the orator, president of the day, the chief marshal, and distinguished friends from abroad, being the happy recipients. Never was there a more pleasing sight. The animated and intelligent faces of these children, their large numbers, stretching a considerable distance along the way, made a beautiful show, and they seemed indeed the jewels of Dorchester. They greeted the distinguished orator and invited guests with the most enthusiastic cheers.

After the procession had passed, the schools joined it, in their order, as follows:—

Col. JOHN P. CLAPP, Marshal.

MATHER SCHOOL—with Banner.

MOTTO—"Mather School, Dorchester. Established 1639." On the reverse, "July 4th, 1855."

Benjamin F. Brown, Principal.

Misses Mary Pearson, Mary M. Smith and Betsey Hooper, Ass'ts.

WINTHROP SCHOOL—with Banner.

MOTTO—"Winthrop School, Dorchester."

Isaac Swan, Principal.

Misses Sophia A. Clapp, E. J. Stetson and S. R. Childs, Ass'ts.

[Scholars belonging to the Eliot Intermediate School, Miss A. French, Teacher; and Primary School, Miss M. Stone, Teacher, were with the Winthrop School.]

GIBSON SCHOOL—with Banner.

MOTTO—"Common Schools—our Country's Hope. Gibson School, July 4, 1855."

Robert Vose, Jr., Principal.

Mrs. M. J. Homer, Misses L. P. Tolman and M. E. Tolman, Ass'ts.

ADAMS SCHOOL—with Banner.

MOTTO—"Adams School, Dorchester." On the reverse side—"'Independence forever.'—Yes, patriot Sire, we will maintain it."

Francis B. Snow, Principal.

Misses Ann Tolman and Kate W. Towne, Ass'ts.

[Scholars belonging to the Maverick School, Misses M. T. Snow and Charlotte W. Towne, Teachers; the Neponset School, Misses L. J. Davis and A. E. Crane, Teachers; and the Stoughton School, Miss M. Larkin, Teacher, were with the Adams School.]

EVERETT SCHOOL—with Banner.

MOTTO—"Everett School, Dorchester. Established 1808."

Robert Richardson, Marshal.

—— ——, Principal.

Misses Jane E. Wate, Mary A. Gleason and J. M. Pratt, Ass'ts.

NORFOLK SCHOOL—with Banner.

MOTTO—"Norfolk School, Dorchester. Common Schools:—
'The tree our Fathers planted, | We'll nourish and protect.'"

Elbridge G. Emery, Principal.

Misses Martha A. Baker and Mary J. Pope, Ass'ts.

[Scholars from the Butler School, Miss Maria Crane, Teacher, were with the Norfolk School.]

BOWDOIN SCHOOL—with Banner.
MOTTO—"Bowdoin School."
Miss Harriet L. Wales, Teacher.

HIGH SCHOOL—with Banner.
MOTTO—"Dorchester High School. July 4, 1855. Possunt quia posse videntur."
On the reverse side—"Dorchester High School, organized Dec. 1852."
William J. Rolfe, Principal.
Misses M. Coburn and Lucy Shepard, Ass'ts.

As these marched into the tent, the scene was most delightful, passing as they did in front of the immense audience, to their seats.

The route of the procession was very tastefully decorated. The decorations were put up by Mr. R. M. Yale, and reflect the highest credit on his taste and judgment.

In front of the house where the distinguished orator of the day was born, there was an arch, trimmed with flags and evergreens. On the span was the inscription,

"THE SCHOLAR AND STATESMAN."

And on the pillars, the following:

| | |
|---|---|
| Born,<br>1794.<br>Entered College at<br>the age of 13.<br>Professor at Harvard<br>at 21.<br>Member of Congress,<br>1824. | Governor of Massachusetts,<br>1835.<br>Minister to England,<br>1841.<br>President of Harvard<br>University, 1846.<br>Secretary of State,<br>1852.<br>U. S. Senator,<br>1853. |

On the limb of a large tree was the inscription—

"BIRTH-PLACE OF EVERETT."

As the procession moved on its way towards the Pavilion, a large number of vehicles of all descriptions, filled with persons, and thousands of others on foot, lined the streets, and indicated their enthusiasm by waving of handkerchiefs, and other demonstrations of joy.

In front of Dea. Ebenezer Clapp's house was the motto,

"THE HOUSE WHERE EVERETT WAS TAUGHT HIS A, B, C.
'Happy is the man that findeth wisdom and the man that getteth understanding.'"

Mr. Samuel B. Peirce's house, and the store of Messrs. A. & J. H. Upham, were handsomely decorated.

Gov. Gardner's residence was also tastefully decorated. In front of it was an arch, handsomely trimmed, at the apex of which was the State Seal; across the span, the motto,

"OLD MASSACHUSETTS AND THE UNION FOREVER."

The pillars of the arch bore the names of the several States, and at their base was the inscription,

"KNOWLEDGE AND THE LAWS."

On the top of the house there was a splendid American flag.

At the entrance to Webster Hill, where the Oration was delivered, was another arch, across the top of which was the inscription,

"DORCHESTER SETTLED IN 1630."

On the pillars were the names of the "Early Settlers," as follows:—

| | |
|---|---|
| Atherton, | Minot, |
| Andrews, | Mather, |
| Blake, | Maverick, |
| Baker, | Robinson, |
| Capen, | Tileston, |
| Clap, | Stoughton, |
| Humphrey, | Sumner, |
| Moseley, | Wales. |

On the reverse, across the top, was the motto,

"DORCHESTER AND HER CHILDREN.

| Milton, | Sharon, | Foxboro', |
|---|---|---|
| Canton, | Stoughton, | Wrentham, |
| | South Boston." | |

The procession reached the tent at about noon, but some time was necessarily occupied in seating the numerous assembly. The ladies had already been admitted. The accommodations were ample, and the audience, numbering scarcely less than five thousand, were easily seated, and presented an imposing aspect. There was a good circulation of air in the tent, and an immense number of palm-leaf fans had been provided for the convenience of the company.

In the tent were displayed the following inscriptions appropriate to the day, selected from the writings of Mr. Everett. On the north side—

"JULY 4th, 1776.
IT IS HENCEFORWARD WHAT THE DYING ADAMS PRONOUNCED IT,
'A GREAT AND GOOD DAY.'"

On the south side of the Pavilion—

"The Hand that traced the Charter of Independence is, indeed, motionless; the eloquent lips that sustained it are hushed; but the lofty spirits that conceived, resolved, and maintained it, and which alone to such men '*make it life* to live,'—these cannot expire."

Hon. Marshall P. Wilder, the President of the day; Hon. Edward Everett, and other gentlemen who were to take part in the services; his Excellency Gov. Gardner (in citizen's dress), accompanied by his four Aids and the Adjutant General (in uniform); Rev. James Walker, D.D., President of Harvard College; Hon. Rufus Choate; Col. Aspinwall, Major Grafton and Gen. Chandler, officers of the war of 1812; Captain Moore and Lieutenant Wise, of the U. S. Navy; Hon. Charles Francis Adams; Prof. Felton, of Cambridge; Hon. Wm. Foster; Hon. Ebenezer Everett, of Brunswick (Me.); Hon. Nathan Hale; the venerable Rev. Dr. Kendall, of Plymouth, Rev. George E. Ellis, Rev. Dr. Frothingham, Rev. Edward Everett Hale, and numerous others of the clergy; Barnas Sears, D.D., Secretary of the Board of Education; Judge Sanger; Judge Hopkinson; several members of the Governor's Council; Hon. Robert B. Hall, M. C.; Hon. Peter Cooper, Hon. Joseph Curtis, Malcolm Ives, Esq., and Rev. Dr. Hosmer, of New York; John Hancock, nephew of Gov. Hancock; Hon. Mr. Hargraves, Factor of the Hudson's Bay Company in North America; I. D. Andrews, Esq., U. S. Consul General for the British Provinces; Arthur W. Austin, Charles Folsom, Richard Frothingham, Jr., Esqs., and a large number of other distinguished gentlemen, occupied seats upon the platform.

The services were commenced with a voluntary by the Boston Brigade Band.

Prayer was offered by Rev. NATHANIEL HALL, of Dorchester.

The following original hymn was sung by one hundred and thirty singers, under the direction of Mr. CHARLES ANSORGE, accompanied by the Band.

## HYMN.

BY REV. S. G. BULFINCH, OF DORCHESTER.

ON the ancestral sod,
Gathered from far abroad,
Thankful we meet;
Many a grassy mound,
In yon old burial ground,
Tells where our sires have found
Rest, calm and sweet.

GOD! who o'er yon blue sea
Guidedst the brave and free
In the old time;
Thanks their descendants pour
That thou did'st lead them o'er
To no soft tropic shore,
But this rough clime.

Thanks, when the destined hour
Of independent power
The ages brought,
That by Thy high command,
A firm and patient band,
Strong heart and valiant hand,
Deliverance wrought.

Nurtured in manly toil,
Tilling a rocky soil,
Pure, free and bold,—
Such praise our fathers bear,
Such may their children share
Save from corruption's snare,
Base lust of gold!

Father and King divine!
On us and on our line
Thy grace be poured!
Union of heart and hand,
Freedom throughout the land,
Strength through all time to stand
True to the Lord!

Mr. JOHN B. TILESTON read the Declaration of Independence.

Hon. MARSHALL P. WILDER, President, next arose and said:—

"Fellow Citizens,—It is not my province to break the seal of your history, or to unwind the roll upon which it is written; but it is my delightful privilege to introduce to you an honored son of Dorchester, one worthy to perform this service, the Hon. EDWARD EVERETT."

Mr. EVERETT was received with the most enthusiastic applause, which was continued for some minutes. When it had subsided, he delivered the preceding eloquent Oration, which was listened to throughout with the most earnest attention. Many passages were greeted with hearty applause. The delivery of the oration occupied two hours and twenty minutes, during which time the distinguished orator did not in a single instance have occasion to refer to his notes.

The following original Ode was sung:

## ODE.

BY REV. N. L. FROTHINGHAM, D.D., OF BOSTON.

Old Dorchester has fame to wear,
Won from the days of Faith and Strife;—
The Faith that winged the Pilgrim's prayer,
The War that breathed a Nation's life.

In front she stood, when first arose
The Church upon the red man's shore;
In front—to meet the shock of foes,
When opened Freedom's cannon roar.

Her heights have felt the foot and eye
Of him who led our victories on;
Her plains run seaward, as to vie
With some yet future Marathon.

Old Dorchester is glad to-day;
Her sacred bells ring feast and mirth;
Her gunner's trains and war-array
But shoot their joy to sky and earth.

Old Dorchester is proud to-day!
Through her own lips its trump is blown;
And he, who speaks what she would say,
By two-fold title is her own.

OLD HUNDRED.

O God of Faith and Armies! now
Make pure our thanks, lift high our vow.
Thy Spirit be thy people's might.
And valor guard their free birthright.

Rev. JAMES H. MEANS, of Dorchester, then offered an appropriate prayer.

## ODE.

BY MISS ANNE S. TILESTON, OF DORCHESTER.

This day unto the breeze again,
Be Freedom's banner proudly flung;
And wave triumphantly as when
Her choral pæan first was sung;
When nations with admiring eyes,
The glorious conflict turned to see,
And watched the star of Peace arise,
When gained our blood-bought Liberty.

Ring out your cadence deep and strong,
Ye joyous bells, with merry peal;
And borne upon the air along,
Let every note be Freedom's seal:
And every Freeman's heart shall beat,
From North to South—on land or sea,
With quicker throb this day to greet,
The day that made our nation free.

How dearly was that freedom bought,
The records of our fathers tell;
Those spirits brave, who, fearing nought,
Against oppression dared rebel,
And with heroic heart and tongue,
They raised the loud, exulting cry;
Through the whole land the chorus rung,
"We will be free—or we will die!"

And in our memory hallowed be
Those patriot souls, who, leaving all,
Gave up their lives for Liberty,
Responsive to their country's call.
A nobler meed on them bestow,
Than sculptured marble can impart;
Let Fame unfading records show,
Inscribed upon a nation's heart.

And ne'er forget the sainted dead,
Who on this great and glorious day—
When Liberty's broad wing was spread,
And Peace spread o'er our land its ray—
In calmness breathed their latest breath,
Midst shout and song, and choral hymn;
Freedom's triumphal hour—their death;
Its jubilee—their requiem.

One chorus let the nation raise,
To hail our country's natal day;
One universal song of praise,
From youth and age ascend alway:
And still while circling ages roll,
Till even time itself is o'er,
The watchword to each freeman's soul,
Be "INDEPENDENCE" evermore.

Shout the glad sound once more,
Let the loud cannon's roar
Echo from shore to shore,
Boom o'er the sea.
Let every nation round,
To earth's remotest bound,
Catch the inspiring sound,
Till all are free.

The services were then closed with the following Benediction, by the Rev. JAMES H. MEANS:—

"The Lord our God be with us, as He was with our Fathers." "The Lord bless you and keep you. The Lord make his face shine upon you, and be gracious unto you. The Lord lift up his countenance upon you and give you peace. *Amen.*"

The Procession was then reformed, under the escort of the Independent Company of Cadets, accompanied by the Weymouth and Boston Brigade Bands. The same order was observed as in its approach to the Pavilion on Webster Hill, with the pleasant addition of numerous ladies, who were to join in the festivities at the dinner table. On its arrival at the Pavilion on Meeting-House Hill, the customary honors were rendered by the Cadets, who paraded in a line on one side, and by a body of United Americans in continental costume, who were stationed on the other side. At the entrance to the tent was a beautifully decorated arch, on which was the following inscription:

"SONS AND DAUGHTERS OF DORCHESTER,
WELCOME HOME."

The procession marched into the tent with the utmost regularity and precision, filing off in regular columns, and taking seats at the tables, which were spread for nearly two thousand persons, and richly furnished with the viands and fruits of the season, by Mr. J. B. Smith, of Boston. They were also ornamented with a profusion of magnificent bouquets from the gardens and conservatories of Dorchester.

The tent was adorned with national emblems, and studded with numerous and appropriate mottoes. The whole scene presented a most interesting and beautiful appearance.

The tables were so arranged as to enable the large audience to see and hear the speakers. On the south side, there was an elevated platform, on which were seated the President and invited guests. On its front, extending the whole length, was the following inscription:—

"PEACE, LIBERTY AND LOVE SHALL CROWN THIS FESTIVE DAY."

On the centre post, directly in front of the President's seat, was the following inscription, surrounded by evergreens and flowers—

MARSHALL P. WILDER,
PRESIDENT OF THE DAY.

"Blessed is he that turneth the waste places into a garden, and maketh the wilderness to blossom as a rose."

On the right of the foregoing was—

"OUR FATHERS TRUSTED IN THEE, AND THOU DIDST DELIVER THEM."

On the left was—

"GOD BE WITH US, AS HE WAS WITH OUR FATHERS."

Opposite the main entrance of the tent was the motto—

"HIS EXCELLENCY HENRY J. GARDNER,
GOVERNOR OF MASSACHUSETTS,
An honored Son of Dorchester."

On the side directly opposite the rostrum, in a conspicuous position, was this motto:—

"NORFOLK COUNTY,
The land of EVERETT and the ADAMSES."

Among the other mottoes were the following:—

"Gov. Winthrop, 1630.
His name and fame still live."

"The good Ship Mary and John in 1630,
and
Train's Packet Ships in 1855."

"Our Country in all that is Great and Good."

"From Ocean's Wave to Ocean's Wave, Perpetual Peace and Friendship."

"Dorchester in 1855.
There is a touch of the Old Puritan about us yet."

"Washington,
The Father of his Country."

"Dorchester Heights and Bunker Hill."

"Edward Everett,
Professor in Harvard College at the age of 21."

"Harvard,
The Alma Mater of the Great and Good of past and present time."

"Our Glorious Constitution, and its Glorious Defender."

"Liberty and Union,
Now and forever, one and inseparable."

"The First Free School Established in Dorchester in 1639."

"Lafayette." "Webster." "Sherman." "Bowdoin."
"Hancock." "Adams." "Franklin."

"In Union is our Strength."

"Enoch Train,
His path is o'er the mountain wave."

"John Bull and Uncle Sam.
May they always live in peace."

"Our March is Onward, and shall not be stayed."

At five o'clock, Maj. Cobb, the Chief Marshal, announced to the President of the day that the Company were all seated, and awaited his pleasure.

Mr. WILDER then rose and said,—

"LADIES AND GENTLEMEN :—It is suitable on all occasions to acknowledge our dependence upon Him who controls the destinies of individuals and nations; especially is it appropriate on this high day of patriotic rejoicing. Let us then unite with the Rev. Mr. Pike, of Dorchester, in imploring the blessing of Heaven on us and on our feast."

The divine blessing was then asked by Mr. PIKE, as follows :—

"Our Father and our God, we thank Thee for this auspicious day; for all its hallowed recollections and interesting associations; we thank Thee for the assembling together from their scattered homes, which this day witnesses, of sons and daughters of this ancient town amid the familiar scenes of their early years, or in the places in which their fathers labored and suffered and hoped in the faith of a Christian people; we thank Thee for this pleasant re-union around these tables spread before us, and for the pleasures of social intercourse to which this hour is consecrated. In partaking of these bounties of Thy hand and in participating in the enjoyments of this occasion, we desire to acknowledge, with grateful hearts, our dependence on Thee for every blessing of our earthly lot, and to have grace given us that we may live henceforth in obedience to the precepts and commandments of Jesus Christ our Saviour. *Amen.*"

After a season spent in the repast, the President called to order, and said :—

"The divine commandment requires that when we have eaten, and are full, we should bless the Lord our God. I will call upon the Rev. Abijah R. Baker, of Lynn, a descendant of Dorchester, to express our thanks."

The Rev. Mr. BAKER returned thanks in the following words :—

"Almighty and most merciful God, we bless thee for these provisions of thy love, for this good land in which we dwell, and for all its institutions, civil, literary and religious. We thank thee for the events which we this day commemorate, for the precious memory of our fathers, and for the rich inheritance which we have received from them, and which, we pray, thy grace may enable us to transmit to our children, and they to theirs till time shall be no more, and thy praise shall be forever perfect in Heaven, through Jesus Christ our Lord. *Amen.*"

Mr. WILDER then arose, amidst applause, and addressed the large assemblage as follows:

*Fellow Citizens, and Descendants of the First Settlers of Dorchester:*

On this seventy-ninth birth-day of our beloved Republic,—on this two hundred and twenty-fifth anniversary of the settlement of our ancient town, I greet you with a right hearty welcome.

In behalf of those whom I have the honor to represent, I tender you our most cordial salutations. Welcome to our festive board. Welcome to the hallowed associations of this day and place. Welcome to our hearts and to our homes, and to all the joys and pleasures of this occasion. [Cheers.]

The time allotted for these exercises demands of me great brevity, nor would I presume to stand between you and those masters of eloquence, from whose lips you are to drink the inspiration of the hour. The story of this day's commemoration is as familiar to you as household words—the landing of our fathers upon these shores—the proclamation of our nation's independence—the erection of the standard of American liberty, and the commencement of her glorious career. [Applause.]

The soil on which we have assembled is consecrated by the recollection of devoted patriotism, and is sanctified by the sacrifices of a noble ancestry. Before us roll the waters which bore on their bosom the good ship Mary and John, freighted with the first settlers of Dorchester. Here were the homes of John Maverick, John Warham, Richard Mather and their godly associates. Here and around us were the homes of Hancock, of Warren, of Prescott, of the Adamses, and other illustrious patriots, who struck some of the first and heaviest blows for freedom, and who consecrated themselves at the altar of liberty, by a baptism of fire and blood. Within our view are Dorchester Heights and Bunker Hill, those everlasting sentinels, which have guarded with sleepless vigilance Massachusetts Bay, in times of awful peril; and there, faithful to their trust, they will stand forever. [Continued cheering.]

*Honored Descendants of Dorchester:* To this home of your patriot sires, we welcome you as the representatives of long and worthy lines, which here had their auspicious beginning; to the spot where the cradle of your infancy was rocked, and where remain the sepulchres in which your fathers still sleep. On this day Dorchester may well rejoice in her sons—in the presence of our elder brother the Orator of the Day and the representative of our nation at the court of Kings [cheers], of our younger brother the Chief Magistrate of the Commonwealth [cheers], and of other worthies among her descendants who have performed honorable service in the councils of our State and nation, the army and navy, in arts and letters, and in morals and religion. We also rejoice in the presence of our neighbors from the various towns which have arisen from the original Dorchester settlement, for the promptness and cordiality with which they have responded to our invitation, especially to the citizens of Boston, a part of whose territory was once the "old cow pasture" of the Dorchester settlers. [Laughter and applause.] *Ladies and Gentlemen*, I intend no reflection upon the Queen city of New England, and she needs no encomium from me. There she stands in her proud pre-eminence, like ancient Rome upon her Capitoline hill. As we gaze at her forests of masts, her crowded and busy marts, her princely dwellings and institutions, and consider her wealth, intelligence and power, we may indulge in a little ancestral pride, for we cannot forget that in the colonial tax of 1633, Dorchester paid £80, or one-fifth of the whole tax, while Boston paid but £48; and that, as history informs us, "Dorchester was the greatest town in New England," but "that Boston was too small to contain many people." [Laughter.] But now that the balance of power has turned, we will glory in her prosperity, and most sincerely do we rejoice to meet our brethren by whom she is here represented. [Cheers.]

*Citizens of Dorchester:* I congratulate you upon the auspicious circumstances under which we meet, upon the flourishing condition of our churches and schools, our efficient fire department, and the various other associations which have united with us to-day —especially upon the presence at this board of so many of our fair matrons and maidens. *Ladies*, we welcome you to a participation in the pleasures of this day. [Great cheering.] Nothing can be more appropriate than your presence, for to you and your patriotic mothers is Dorchester much indebted for its celebrity and welfare.

But I must not trespass upon the indulgence of this assembly. One word more, and I will proceed to introduce to you the distinguished guests I see around me, and who, inspired by the surpassing eloquence of the orator of the day, are no doubt waiting to give utterance to the excited emotions of their hearts. To them I cheerfully accord the privilege of gleaning after this great reaper. Sheaves they can hardly expect to find; but if they should chance to gather a few grains, I trust they will give us the results of their labors.

*Friends and Fellow Citizens:* We stand here upon the broad platform of American citizenship, to rejoice in the glorious principles of our fathers, and to perpetuate by the services of this day their precious memories. But how wonderful the contrast between their sacrifices, and the priceless blessings we enjoy; between the glimmering fires of liberty which they kindled on these shores, and the light and glory of this latter day; between the Mattapan of 1630, with its few feeble colonists just landed at "Old Harbor," and this goodly Dorchester in 1855, the mother of a quarter of a million of sons and daughters! [Loud applause.]

And whose soul does not glow with patriotic and grateful feelings at the recollection of these events,—events which have made this nation the most intelligent, free and happy on earth, and which are fast revolutionizing the world,—events which constitute the sublimest facts of history, and which in their results transcend the powers of human understanding. [Sensation.] And who does not feel an interest in this day's commemoration? Whose heart has not been affected by the scenes of this day; the peal of merry bells, the booming of cannon, the sight of congregated thousands, and by the thought of twenty-five millions of happy freemen uniting to swell the pæan of American Freedom, and to offer up, as with the voice of many waters, their hallelujahs and thanksgivings to the God of Nations! [Repeated cheers.]

The President then announced the first toast.

*The Day we Celebrate*—Fraught with precious memories of deliverance from oppression,—bright with glorious anticipations of freedom for the world. [Cheers.]

The second sentiment was:—

*The United States of America*—ONE AND INSEPARABLE: NOW AND FOREVER! [Enthusiastic applause.]

To this toast it was expected the Hon. RUFUS CHOATE would have responded, but the state of his health prevented him from being at the dinner table. [See his letter and article in Appendix.]

THE PRESIDENT.—It is a source of great gratification, that among Dorchester's distinguished sons, it is our privilege to recognize, on this occasion, the Chief Magistrate of our beloved Commonwealth. I propose as a sentiment:

*Massachusetts*—The chosen land of our Puritan Fathers. She was the first to strike for liberty; she will be the last to desert its standard. [Cheers.]

The President then introduced His Excellency HENRY J. GARDNER, who was received with rounds of applause. The Governor responded as follows:—

*Mr. President, Ladies and Gentlemen:*

I am glad at all times to recognize, and bear witness to, the truth of the sentiment you, Sir, have just announced, complimentary to Massachusetts. Yet, now, in this place, at home as I am, I can but feel that propriety and true politeness dictate that I should occupy but little of your time, while others, strangers and gentlemen of eloquence and fame, are yet to be heard.

Were it not so, however, I should distrust my power to fix your attention after the affluent intellectual banquet of the morning. Ours has to-day been a rare privilege, and while listening to the eloquent orator, I could not but think that though he portrayed so beautifully events and scenes of historic and local pride to Dorchester, yet he himself was a source of as just pride to her as any of them all. His character and attainments surpass even his own felicitous delineaments of her social, intellectual and moral advantages.

It is true that this ancient town was settled before our metropolis,—was intended by its founders as the capital of the Province,—and for some period surpassed or rivalled at least Boston. But when the fiat went forth, and Boston took the lead of Dorchester in numbers and in wealth, it was owing to a large portion of her citizens voluntarily leaving this their new town, and on account of commercial facilities migrating to the peninsula of

Shawmut. Yet though depleted by emigration, dismembered into a half dozen separate municipalities, and even now, once and again diminished by annexation to the adjacent City, Dorchester has constantly continued, for two centuries and a quarter, prosperous and increasing.

And to-day, in all her glory, she welcomes her returning sons. From Cow-pasture Bar to Pine-Garden Rock, from Neponset River to Roxbury Brook, she bids them welcome. Change, they may find, has worked its ravages on much around them,—the brow may be somewhat furrowed with weightier cares, the look somewhat graver with sterner duties, but the same warm heart beats within, and sends forth, as of yore, its cordial greeting.

But remembering my promise, I close by proposing as a sentiment,—

That Civil and Religious Liberty which our ancestors sought these shores to secure, which has been preserved through toils and privations by our fathers: May we fulfil our whole duty in aiding to perpetuate it to coming generations. [Applause.]

The President then said—The sentiment which I am about to propose I am sure will call forth a cordial response from this assembly. Nor are any words of mine necessary to assure the distinguished gentleman to whom it alludes, of the great satisfaction his presence affords to the citizens of Dorchester, and the thousands who have assembled this day to hear his voice. He then gave—

*The Orator of the Day.*—Dorchester recognizes in him her ripest Scholar, her profoundest Statesman, and her most eloquent Orator. She delights to honor a son who has reflected so much honor upon her.

This sentiment was received with nine hearty cheers, the company all standing.

Mr. Everett, in response, made the following felicitous speech.

*Mr. President, Ladies and Gentlemen:*

I need not tell you how grateful I am to you all for this most cordial welcome. I wish the state of my voice, after the effort of the morning, would allow me to express my feelings more audibly and at more appropriate length. If the kind language that you have been pleased to use toward me, could lead me so far to flatter myself, as to think I was capable of saying any good thing at any time, it would but the more forcibly impress upon me, at this time, the truth of the old maxim, that there may be too much even of a good thing. [Laughter.]

I feel that to-day I have already had my full share of the time and the attention of this most intelligent company; and I should reproach myself, Sir, if I could presume so far upon your kind encouragement, as to intrude myself upon them much longer, even if I were capable of doing so, in my present state of physical exhaustion.

But grateful as I am, Mr. President, for the kind notice you have taken of me, you will allow me to say that, in your opening address, there was one allusion, on which you will permit me a single remark. There was a little significance, I thought, which might have been spared, in what you said of our "elder brother." [Laughter.] Now, Sir, I am not so discourteous as to hint, that the President of the day could, at any time, make an intimation without matter of fact to support it; and if the truth must be told, I fear it will turn out, that I am somewhat his "elder brother." But I must say that your use of the epithet, and the obliging smile which accompanied it [laughter], brought to my mind an anecdote of one of the predecessors of His Excellency the Governor, in the olden times. I refer to Gov. Strong.

Gov. Strong was holding a council with a deputation of Stockbridge Indians, who used occasionally to come down to Boston, to pay their respects to their "great father," and solicit a little "material aid." Governor Strong, in the course of his "talk," said to them, with bland condescension, "Our hearts are of the same color, though our faces are lighter than yours." Now it so happenėd that Governor Strong was a man of very dark complexion—very. And when this expression fell from his lips, the leader of the Indians was observed, as he stood at the other side of the Council chamber, to show some signs of impatience, and to murmur something in a low voice. The Governor paused in his address, and asked an officer who stood near, what the chief was saying. The person interrogated, replied, with some reluctance and hesitation, "Why, your Excellency, he says, he does not think there is much difference in the color of their faces;—'not mush,' as he calls it." [Great laughter.] So, Mr. President, with respect to our ages, to which you have so obligingly alluded, I do not think there is "much difference." [Laughter.] Some eight or ten years, perhaps; but what is that to make a talk about before two thousand friends? [Laughter.]

The Governor said I had omitted one thing in my oration, and that was that a considerable number of Dorchester people had gone over to Boston, at an early period of the settlement. But that was a point I did not like to say much about; it is one of some delicacy with me. I knew a Dorchester boy, in later times, —a very dutiful son of our ancient town, who also ran away to Boston. [Laughter.] And I can only say that I am pretty sure he sometimes wishes he was well back again. [Renewed laughter.]

Again, Mr. President, allow me to say that I am greatly indebted to you and our friends around me for this most kind reception. It is not the first time I have dined on Meeting-house Hill, though it is certainly the first time I have had the honor of dining here in a company like this. But in old-fashioned times, fifty or sixty years ago, when the little boys came a long way from home in mid-winter to school, and their fathers and mothers did not think they ought to travel the distance four times a day, they were fitted out, in bad weather, with a dinner to be eaten at school. It was called "Staying at noon." We were provided with a basket, in which was a little bread and cheese, or a piece of cold meat, an apple, a sausage, sometimes uncooked, to be roasted on the end of a stick at the school stove; not greatly to the benefit of the air of the school-room. That was the dinner: there were none of those niceties which now load our tables; no chicken salads, no ice creams, no strawberries, no delicacies of any kind, no bright faces of the fairer half of creation, no banners, no music; no joyous demonstrations; but good old Dorchester school-boy fare.

Alas, such times can be lived over but once, Mr. President. We can never be young but once. That is impossible! But the best we can do, when we cease to be young, and find ourselves verging toward the decline of life, is to take pleasure in the company of our "younger brethren." [Laughter.] Happy as I am at finding myself at the side of one so much my junior, I will only, in taking my seat, express the heart-felt wish for the welfare of every lady and gentleman present, and the continued growth and prosperity of our beloved native Dorchester. [Long-continued applause.]

The next toast was,—

*The Descendants of Dorchester*—Their name is legion, their home everywhere. We welcome them to-day to the land of their fathers. Dorchester is not only proud of her children, but of her children's children. Honor to those who honor their parents. [Cheers.]

The President called upon the Rev. EDWARD EVERETT HALE, a descendant of Dorchester, to respond to this sentiment. Mr. Hale said:—

I think, Sir, that we, who are the children's children, if not most at home here to-day, are most at ease. We can compliment every-thing we see, and can join in the compliments we hear, without making modest exceptions while we speak, and without blushing while we listen. Indeed, Sir, just as we are all proud that we were born of such mothers as we are, we have reason to be proud of our grand-mother Dorchester. [Cheers.]

I do not think, Sir, that we recognize the full value of the debt we owe the fathers whose names you have hung up all around us to-day, precisely because the result of their work has made these old homes of theirs so beautiful. We have a feeling that any body might have been glad to emigrate to America,—particularly just now, when so large a body of you young Americans are making attempts for "obstructing the laws for the naturalization of foreigners." We do not, I say, reflect, how many Emigrant Aid Companies it needed to bring hither Warham and Maverick and Mather, the men of whom we have been hearing to-day. Dorchester, as we see it, is such a lovely place, that we think it a very excellent thing to get here. [Cheers.] They thought it much the same thing as you would think it to remove yourself to the head of the Republican Fork, or to settle yourself in one of the parks of the Rocky Mountains. It happens, however, that we know just the valuation put on this continent by England, when England got hold of it. These settlers came under English law, to a region which the kings of England claimed by right of discovery. Against France and against Spain they asserted their right to the whole of North America, because an English sailor had discovered it. Now, what did the king of England give him for his discovery? When the hard-faced old Cabot,—ancestor of your Cabot,—went home to the king of England, and told him that he had discovered North America, what did the king say to him? We have the king's account-book of that day's expenses. In that book there are these items:—

| | |
|---|---|
| "To the damsel that danceth, . . . . . . . . . . . . | £12 |
| To the man who found the new island, . . . . . . . . . | £10 |
| To Jake Haute, for tennis play, . . . . . . . . . . . | £9 |
| To a woman with a red rose, . . . . . . . . . | 2 shillings." |

The Continent of North America was rated less than a dance, and cost the crown of England just the price of a hundred red roses! [Laughter and applause.]

Well, Mr. President, this was three or four hundred years ago. But sometimes when I have looked in upon our monarchs of horticulture, when I have seen some of your garden-princes, comparing your *Gloria Rosamundi*, your *Souvenir de Malmaison*, or your dear old *Hermosa*, I have fancied then, that if a hard-faced old fellow should come in and say, "I have found you an island in the salt sea of Utah, what will you give me for it?" and a woman, yes, a woman, Sir, with a new red rose, more beautiful than *Gloria Rosamundi*,—you would give her two shillings for her red rose, before you would give him ten pounds for his island! *That* was what the king of England did. [Cheers.]

The origin of that emigration, Sir, to lands thus slighted, is of particular interest to the ministers of Massachusetts. It has been particularly grateful, this day, to hear the eulogy passed on that minister, Rev. John White, of Old Dorchester, not only the founder of this town, but the founder of Massachusetts and so of Connecticut. All that Massachusetts and Connecticut have done, we owe in its origin, under the providence of God, to John White, minister of Dorchester. I was glad to hear this made so clear to-day, in a time when it seems to be sometimes expected that ministers shall not attempt to found anything at all. That town of his, Old Dorchester, of which he was the patriarch, was called, I think by Clarendon, the magazine of rebellion,—"*the magazine whence the other places were supplied with the principles of rebellion.*" When they ran short of *principles* in London, or in the

North, or in the East, they sent to the Dorchester magazine for a new supply. [Applause.] The sneer of that day is the glory of this day for Old Dorchester. The principles of constitutional liberty are scattered over the world: an honor to the old town, that she was the magazine of those principles, when magazine there was but one. And this new Dorchester of ours has lived to see something of the same experience. After our defeat at Lexington, for it was a defeat; after the defeat at Concord, for it was a defeat; after the defeat at Bunker Hill, for it was a defeat;—Dorchester Heights witnessed that "more than victory," which has to-day been described to us—the victory commemorated in the first medal of our minted history, with its proud motto, *Hostibus primo fugatis:* the first rout of the enemy. The country was at the moment of its despair; and all over the country, from here to our friends in Georgia, Dorchester Heights threw the first sparks of encouragement and hope. Old Dorchester and young Dorchester,—for we are young, after all,—have had this common experience; and I will give you for a sentiment:—

Old Dorchester, the magazine of principles when English constitutional liberty was young; new Dorchester, the first scene of victory when American constitutional liberty was young—May the omens of the past rule the history of the future. [Applause.]

THE PRESIDENT.—It affords me great pleasure to announce, that we are honored by the presence of the President of Harvard University, and I propose for your consideration, as a sentiment:—

*Harvard College*—Our forefathers, knowing that freedom could not be maintained without education, founded that institution as the safeguard of human rights. More than two hundred years has she been faithful to her trust, and she still stands a rock of defence against ignorance and superstition. [Cheers.]

Rev. JAMES WALKER, D.D., President of the University, responded to this sentiment in the following felicitous speech.

*Mr. President, Ladies and Gentlemen:*

Harvard College has been called the High School of Boston and the neighboring towns. I believe the name is commonly given in a tone of disparagement; but I see no reason why the friends of the College should disown the truth which has suggested it. No college in this country leans so much on the surrounding community as ours does; and no college has such a surrounding community on which to lean; and furthermore, it is glory enough for Harvard College to be considered as one among the instrumentalities which have made this community what it is. I do not forget how much we owe to our ancient and beloved Commonwealth, and to the whole country; but our principal indebtedness is to the surrounding community: there is hardly a historical name of this group of cities and towns which is not enrolled among the benefactors of the College. [Applause.]

To Dorchester, Harvard College is under peculiar obligations. Who can remain for a single day within the precincts of the College, and not hear the name of Stoughton?—one of the oldest and most distinguished of the Dorchester names. The Stoughtons, both father and son, were among the earliest and most liberal benefactors of the College; the son, by far its largest benefactor in the seventeenth century, if we except Harvard himself. [Cheers.] But this is not our only, or our chief debt of gratitude to Dorchester. In our own days she has given us a student whose scholarship is the pride of his country. [Applause.] A son of Harvard, who has reflected the highest honor on the place of his education in every situation he has filled throughout his various and honored life [applause]; and a President, the wisdom and efficiency of whose administration will be felt and acknowledged as long as the College stands. [Hearty applause.]

THE PRESIDENT.—*Ladies and Gentlemen*—We have present, I am happy to say, many distinguished friends, upon whom I shall call in order, should time permit. But I have now to offer a sentiment, to which I think the gentlemen will at least respond. It was customary, in olden time, to save the best wine until the last; and consequently the sentiment to the ladies was reserved until then. But I propose now to reverse that order, and I give you:—

*Woman*—Earth's fairest flower. Without her, home is "Paradise Lost"; with her, home is "Paradise Regained." [Received with nine cheers. Music by the Band and Orchestra, with one stanza of "Home, Sweet Home."]

Col. ENOCH TRAIN rose, amid many cheers, and said:—According to parliamentary usage, an amendment to a motion is allowable. I have one to offer to that elegant sentiment which we have just heard from your lips, Mr. President. It is mathematical, and refers to the ladies, who are all mathematical, thank God! [Laughter and merriment.]

*The Ladies*—
May they *add* Virtue to Beauty;
*Subtract* Envy from Friendship;
*Multiply* amiable accomplishments by sweet temper;
*Divide* time by sociability and economy—
And *reduce* Scandal to its lowest denomination. [Great applause.]

THE PRESIDENT.—*Ladies and Gentlemen*—It is our good fortune to-day, to have with us a lineal descendant of two Presidents of the United States, the Adamses, to the elder of whom it has been truly said, "we owe our independence more than to any other created being"; and of the younger it may be said, with equal propriety, that he labored longer than any other man of his generation, for the preservation of that independence. I give you as a toast:—

*Our Guest from Quincy*—The son, the grandson and the historian of these patriot sires. Long may he live, to gather the rich harvest of their planting. [Applause.]

Hon. CHARLES FRANCIS ADAMS replied in the following eloquent speech:—

*Mr. President:*

I owe you many thanks for the honor you have done me, by inviting me to respond to the last sentiment. Permit me to say that I am a little overcome by it. With the recollections that cluster about this day, we may all, without exception, be allowed to express somewhat loudly our gratitude to past generations for the blessings which we now enjoy through their labors. Yet if the indulgence of this sentiment imparts satisfaction, it does not the less awaken serious reflection. The event of 1776 inaugurated a new thought into the politics of the world. And this thought was so far cherished in America as to harden into action through our institutions. It was not merely a revival of the ancient notion of national liberty. The impression is not uncommon among us, even now, that a release from the rule of Great Britain was all that was contemplated by the struggle. But this seems to me to be giving a narrow view of its nature and purposes. Surely the men of that day, besides providing security for individual freedom, meditated a system resting upon the indispensable duty of self-control, as well as a wide diffusion of knowledge, high moral excellence and political purity; all, elements of the best state to which man on earth can aspire, that of a *great Christian Commonwealth.* That they did not fully attain their objects, I am not prepared to deny. The obstacles were great, and they had perpetual interruptions, extrinsic in their nature, to distract their attention. Yet it may be fairly claimed for them that they accomplished much, before the inevitable hour came which put a stop to their labors. In the movements of nations we must all remember that a generation is but a span. And still further, that what they had no time to do, it therefore devolves upon us their successors yet to complete. The responsibility is not upon them, but upon us. We assume their places under trials not less severe, though of a wholly opposite nature. If theirs came from the endurance of adversity, ours spring from the enervating influence of continual temporal blessings. Whether we shall be as worthy of praise for overcoming the internal weakness of the heart, as they were for their triumph over the assaults of external oppressors, it remains for time to prove. If we do, then is our course plain and straightforward to the goal which they marked out. If we do not, the effect will be to dissipate their great purposes into thin air, or perhaps to suffer ourselves to be diverted to others of quite an opposite character. [Cheers.]

But if I am asked how this responsibility of ours is to be fully discharged, my answer is clear. It can only be fully done by maintaining in our own bosoms that sacred fire, the aspiration for all that is truly high and noble, which animated them. Wanting this, all our multitudinous assemblages to celebrate this occasion are but a vain show; the pomp and display of rejoicing, but empty ceremony. The temple of our government may be grand and imposing to the outward eye, the sacrifices at the public altar may be as costly and splendid as money can buy; if the heart is not there to give the vital heat, they will be of no avail to redeem the future from dishonor. If I may be allowed to compare great things with small, I would illustrate my view by reminding you of those undertakings to improve our domestic communications which have of late become so familiar to us every where. In prosecuting these, the mountains have been cut down and the valleys have been filled up, and long curves of the earth's surface have been bound with iron ways. Yet all this is of no use—the most complete apparatus of motion which the ingenuity of man has ever devised fails to carry us to the destined point, if the Promethean spark of fire be not applied. Grant but this to rouse the expansive force of what in former days passed for another element, water, and the great machine is at once in movement, directed by the hand of man steadily and surely to its destination. And just so it is with the grander moral movement of our republican system. If it be not continually stirred by the fire of *progressive zeal* developing the expandible water of conservative *fidelity to trust*, all the efforts and all the aspirations of our excellent ancestors must prove at last but labor in vain. [Applause.]

Reflecting on this topic, my thoughts naturally led me from the consideration of what duty required to be done, towards a not less important thought, what it would be wisdom to avoid. Involuntarily my eyes turned to the scenes now enacting on the other side of the ocean, and to the very different manner in which great nations there were engaged in spending this day. Without a wish to enter into the merits of their dispute, I content myself with noting what appear to be the ultimate objects of the contending parties, and comparing them with those suggested by the reminiscences of this day. The orator, whose eloquent voice is yet fresh in our ears, gave us a striking and a just idea of the consternation that overspread all Christendom upon the occasion of the triumph of the followers of Mahomet the Second over the defences of Constantinople. Four hundred years have since passed away, and the land, which was won by the sword, has remained under the sword, a land of moral and political desolation. Yet the chief purpose of one party to the present strife is to keep up for an indefinite future the very same state of things which has so long prevailed in the past; to uphold the power of the Crescent over the Cross in the very cradle of Christianity itself. So, on the other hand, if we truly comprehend the motives of the opposite side, its victory would end only in the annexation of another wide tract of earth to an empire already suffering from the denial to its inhabitants of the noblest privileges which belong to the human race. Thus, whichever way we look, designs like these excite in us no sympathy. Already have at least two hundred thousand brave men laid down lives which might have passed in making the land now whitened with their bones a very garden of Eden, in the futile effort to keep a balance of power which has no weights more solid than mutual jealousies and reciprocal preventions. In such a picture I look in vain for heroism or for motives truly admirable. Yet perhaps a single class of exceptions may be made. The veritable hero of this war is, after all, *a woman*. [Cheers.] Nay, with perfect respect for the achievement of Miss Nightingale, I cannot set beneath it the moral force of the example of those more humble sisters of charity, who are described, in the very midst of the thunders of the enemy's artillery, the crash of surrounding edifices, and the wailings of the dying, as not diverted from the duty to which they have cheerfully devoted their lives, of watching and praying by the couches of the fallen. In these acts are the symptoms of a higher life, but no where else. All the rest will serve as a warning to us in America to discern what we should avoid ; as a lesson teaching us to subdue passions, the indulgence of which leads only to bitter results, and never to swerve in our devotion to the principles set forth by the wisdom and the patriotism of the founders of these States. [Applause.]

Let me conclude my remarks by proposing, in the form of a sentiment, a summary of the whole matter. It is this—

The *true* balance of power, among citizens, within states, and between nations ;—Fidelity to trust, before God and man. [Cheers.]

The next sentiment was—

*Our Representation in Congress*—While guarding our material interests, may they express our love of liberty and our loyalty to the Constitution. [Applause.]

Hon. Robert B. Hall, of Plymouth, Representative from the 1st District, was expected to respond, but had been compelled by an engagement to leave the pavilion. Dr.

BARNAS SEARS, Secretary of the Massachusetts Board of Education, was then called upon, and spoke as follows:

*Mr. President :*

I suppose it is not expected that I shall respond for Congress. [*President*—No, Sir, you are expected to speak as Secretary of the Board of Education.] The Common School, then, which I have the honor to represent, is fitly included in the celebration of this day, and its appearance in the procession has added to the beauty and interest of the scene. It had its part in the early history of the colony, and it was intimated by the orator of the day that, *possibly*, to Dorchester belonged the honor of establishing the first school in the colony. Many cities and towns claim that honor; and if they show themselves worthy of it, we may admit the claim on the ground that, whether true or not, it ought to be true. The schools of Dorchester are known to be worthy of such an origin. [Applause.] The schools of Massachusetts have done their full share in making her what she is. The free district school was of itself an important institution—was one of the pillars of the State. But the most important thing was the spirit with which it was maintained. Into it was infused, at the outset, and ever after, the genius of a Christian civilization,—a civilization which was the growth of ages. Greece had developed the human mind with reference to politics, literature and art, but without a knowledge of the divine plan in respect to the end of human existence. Rome had defined the rights of the individual in a wonderful system of law, and by conquest diffused this legal spirit over the civilized world; and yet Rome never knew the true value of the human soul, nor the ground of its claim to liberty. Education, in these ancient seats of honor and refinement, could not rise above the principle on which it was founded.

The Christianity of the early and middle ages furnished the first corrective, but blindly excluded ancient culture as a component part of a complete Christian education. Still an intensity was given to the longings and activity of the human mind by means of its contact with spiritual and eternal things, which prepared it, on its reunion with ancient culture by the revival of learning, to produce what never before existed, a civilization flowing from Christianity as its source, but running in channels opened and prepared by Greece and Rome. [Cheers.] The swelling stream of Christianity, making all former and all contemporary progress tributary to itself,—this it was which, by a Providential arrangement, came to our fathers at the very time that the institutions of the old world checked its free course, and the new world was thrown open with its larger and freer channels of communication. All previous history was necessary to prepare the colonists for founding our free States. No other people could be educated in the same spirit. It was because our fathers were true to their high trust, with lofty views and aims, striving to usher in a better period, that succeeding generations have been educated and trained for the service required of them in the cause of humanity. The essential condition of success in our schools *now* is the keeping up in our minds of this pure ideal of human society. [Cheers.] We must instil into the minds of the young, ideas of a higher and purer life, and make them feel that there is a great work for them and their posterity to achieve, which was impossible in former years; that all the past has been slowly accumulating knowledge and inventing means and instruments for them to employ in advancing to a still higher degree the well-being of society.

The mere mechanical drill of the school-room, the daily toil of the teacher in giving the elements of knowledge, will not advance society unless the social atmosphere breathed by the young be healthful and invigorating. The family educates; the social circle educates; the political press educates; literature educates; fashion educates; the public assembly educates; we this day educate. Unless all these teachings tend in the right direction, it will be in vain that we trust in our schools for safety. The schools receive their character from the people. You have tenfold more power over teacher and pupil than they have over you, and can more effectually prevent the good they would do, than they the evil you may do. Create, then, a pure moral atmosphere for your schools. Let the town and the neighborhood be free from contamination, and then it will not reach the school. Let the love of freedom, of virtue and of religion everywhere be manifest, and then a new generation will be trained up in our schools, with all the care that is now bestowed upon them, to whom it will be safe, with God's blessing, to commit the sacred interests which we so tenderly cherish in our hearts this day. [Applause.]

THE PRESIDENT.—I am happy to state that we are honored with the presence of a delegation of Officers of the Army of 1812. I propose as a sentiment—

*The Army*—Born amid the fires of the Revolution, and trained on the battle fields of our country. Though small, the myriad hosts of Europe can boast no brighter fields, or more glorious achievements. [Cheers.]

The President then introduced Col. THOMAS ASPINWALL, late U. S. Consul at London, who responded as follows:

*Mr. President:*

I have a deep sense of the honor done me by your call to respond to the toast in compliment to the Army. But, I fear, the call is open to two objections: first, that by my long separation from that body, I am hardly entitled to speak for it; and next, that from long habits of silence on such occasions, I have lost all aptitude for public speaking.

But I still retain a sufficiently clear recollection and impression of military feeling and character to assure you, Sir, that the compliment, just paid to the Army, by such an assemblage, will not fail to meet with a respectful and hearty welcome. [Applause.] For the soldier naturally looks to the approbation of his fellow citizens, as the great object of his hopes. It mingles with his dreams. It sustains and cheers him in hardship and danger. It stimulates him to the severest personal sacrifices and to court the most arduous and perilous enterprises; and, if he fail to gain the good opinion of those, for whom he is ready to lay down his life, he feels it, always, as a disappointment and a mortification, but often, as the heaviest of misfortunes, "a stain" worse than "a wound." [Cheers.]

The military spirit of this country, whenever called forth, whether to repel or chastise the incursion of the savage Indian, or to fight the battles of the mother country in this Western Hemisphere, or in the subsequent contests of the Revolution and more recent periods, has always, in the eyes of the world, been honorable to the nation; and on this great anniversary of our national freedom, it is well to remember that those, who were most instrumental in gaining for us that freedom, have left us a rich legacy in the example of their own character and conduct, in their spirit of lofty patriotism, of noble and generous self-sacrifice, of zealous and untiring perseverance in the deadly struggle for the common cause, for the country's welfare, for *national* freedom and independence. [Cheers.] They have left us models of character, worthy to be studied and copied by every military man; and if our official men and political aspirants throughout the breadth of the land, should habitually recur to these models for guidance, it would go far to improve their sentiments, conduct and usefulness, and at the same time to raise the standard of our moral and political character.

As the existing army of the United States is now a component part of the general system established by law, and being, myself, no longer connected with it, I may be permitted to say, that the advantages of academical instruction and discipline which it enjoys, have raised it to a degree of efficiency, much superior to that of previous periods, and also, to a high rank, in the opinion of competent military judges abroad. As a signal instance of this estimation, I would add, that the late Duke of Wellington, no mean authority, pronounced the march of General Scott to Mexico, with his inconsiderable force, in spite of the difficulties of the landing and route, to be one of the military miracles of the age. [Applause.]

The next sentiment was—

*The Navy*—The ocean attests her valor. Although she now rests safely moored in the harbor of peace, let but the enemy awake her, and her thunders will startle the nations. [Cheers.]

THE PRESIDENT.—*Ladies and Gentlemen*—I think I cannot proceed farther without the "benefit of clergy." I will therefore give you—

*The Clergy*—The pioneers of the Revolution—may they be the conservators of the liberty it achieved. [Cheers.]

To this sentiment, Rev. LYMAN WHITING, Chaplain of the Senate, responded eloquently, maintaining the conservatism of the clergy and their influence for good, both in the church and state. He concluded with the following toast:

*The Clergy as Pioneers of the Revolution were helped by patriotic Parishioners*—May they ever find patriotic parishioners to help them preserve the liberty of the country. [Cheers.]

LEWIS PIERCE, Esq., of Dorchester, one of the Vice Presidents, asked permission to propose a toast, and gave—

*The President of the Day*—Distinguished throughout the nation as the friend of Agriculture and Rural Art. Whatever he touches he adorns. Dorchester claims him as her adopted son.

This sentiment was received with three times three cheers.

Mr. WILDER responded as follows:

*Ladies and Gentlemen:*

I tender you my heart-felt acknowledgments for the cordial greetings with which you have received the sentiment announced by our worthy Vice President; but had I known his object, perhaps I might not have so readily yielded the floor to him. I beg, however, to say, that if I have been enabled to perform any service for you or for my country, at all worthy of this compliment, I owe it quite as much to your kind adoption, and to the support of my fellow citizens, as to any ability of mine. [Cheers.] No one rejoices in the prosperity of Dorchester, of our Commonwealth, and of our Republic, more than I do, or looks forward to the bright future with more glorious anticipations. But who can foretell their progress and renown, when two hundred and twenty-five years more shall have completed their course! Ere that day shall dawn, we shall have been gathered to our fathers; but other millions will then celebrate the birth-day of American Freedom. That the influences of this day's commemoration may live to bless our children and our children's children, to the latest generation, is my earnest prayer and hope. [Applause.]

The President then alluded to the complimentary service performed by the Independent Company of Cadets, and gave:

*Our Military Escort—the Independent Company of Cadets*—The right arm of His Excellency the Commander in Chief, and the entrenched guard of the Commonwealth—A model of citizen soldiery. [Hearty cheers.]

Col. THOMAS C. AMORY, Commander of the Cadets, having left the pavilion when this sentiment was given, has since kindly sent the following note in response.

To the inhabitants of Dorchester, through you, Mr. President, and their Committee, the Cadets are indebted for the honor of an invitation on this memorable day, which to us has been an occasion of much pleasure. For your kind complimentary notice of the corps, and for all the attention which has been bestowed on our comfort and enjoyment, I beg leave to return you our sincere thanks. For whatever may have appeared praiseworthy in the movements or discipline of the corps, we are in a great measure indebted to the instructions of Lieut. Colonel James W. Sever, our former commander and a resident in Dorchester, and for the remainder to the members themselves, for their self-sacrificing spirit and unremitting exertions to make themselves proficient in their military exercises.

Mr. President, my own associations with Dorchester have been somewhat peculiar, as well as pleasant. In my boyhood I was often among you, residing with my relatives, and during that period it was my privilege to listen to religious instruction from the lips of that excellent man, the Rev. Dr. Harris. I was also for some time under the tuition of Mr. Elisha Clapp, a Dorchester man, who fitted me for College. He was a most faithful and excellent instructor, and a strict disciplinarian, and had a peculiar faculty of making his *dull* boys *smart* in the *end*.

In College I became acquainted and lived under the same roof with the learned and eloquent orator of the day, who has so much enlightened and delighted us, and for whom I entertain the highest personal respect—so that my early associations with Dorchester and its inhabitants have been of the most pleasant and agreeable description.

Mr. President, there is in this assemblage a member of the Cadets, whom we are proud to claim as "one of ours," and who to-day so well served you in the honorable and responsible position of Chief Marshal. This gentleman is at the head of one of the most important arms of military service, and to it in fact may be fairly attributed much of the success which crowned the efforts of our national armies, against most fearful odds, in the late war with Mexico—I mean the Light Artillery. By his energy and skill he has in this Commonwealth brought it to a degree of perfection which reflects the highest honor on himself and his associates.

And now, Mr. President, I will no longer trespass on your time, but offer you as a sentiment—

*The* EVENT *we celebrate and its consequent* BLESSINGS.—They who evince no interest in the *first*, hardly deserve to participate in the *others*.

THE PRESIDENT.—*Ladies and Gentlemen*—We have among our honored guests from the City of New York, one, who has devoted a large fortune, nearly half a million of dollars I believe, in establishing institutions for the diffusion of knowledge. I refer to Hon. Peter Cooper, the munificent founder of the Cooper Institute in New York. [Cheers.]

Mr. COOPER responded as follows:

*Mr. President, and Gentlemen:*

After the eloquent remarks to which we have listened with so much pleasure, it would be improper for me to occupy your time in the presence of so many gentlemen, who are altogether more able to interest you than myself. Your kind allusion to my humble efforts to advance the cause of science, claims from me a reply, that I fear it will be entirely out of my power to offer. I will venture, however, so far as to assure you, that if the institution to which reference has been made, shall accomplish but a small part of the good that I desire, it will amply compensate for all efforts that have been required to give it a permanent and useful existence. It has fallen to my lot, Mr. President, to know just enough of the beauties and benefits of scientific knowledge to awaken within me an inextinguishable desire to spread its blessings throughout the world. [Cheers.] If I am not mistaken, Mr. President, it is to the spread of knowledge, and a right application of the exact sciences to all the varied uses and purposes of life, that we must look for all future improvement in the condition of mankind. I mean such an application and use of science as will so unveil the wonderful and beautiful mysteries of creation, that "What may be known of God will be clearly seen, being understood by that which he has made." I indulge the hope that a right application and use of scientific knowledge will yet elevate man to comprehend the true dignity of his nature, and the powers given him, by which it is both our privilege and duty to keep, subdue and have dominion over the great garden of the world, and thus demonstrate that the right use of every thing is good, and that the wrong use of anything is an evil—an evil destined by the operations of an immutable law to afflict us as individuals, as communities, as States and nations, not willingly but of necessity; for our profit, so "filling us with our own ways," making us sick of our sins, and willing to yield obedience to those laws and principles of eternal truth and justice. [Applause.] Laws that will finally in their operations reward every man according to his works, and that without respect to persons. I will not longer occupy your time, only to thank you for the honor you have conferred, by inviting me to join you in celebrating the birth of our national independence. With your permission I will offer the following sentiment:—

*The Day we Celebrate*—May every return strengthen the bonds that bind together our union of States in perpetual and fraternal interest and affection. [Applause.]

Mr. Ebenezer Clapp, Jr. being called upon for a speech, furnished the following paper:—

*Mr. President:*

The question why the early settlers of this part of Massachusetts selected Mattapan for their abode, has no doubt entered the mind of many, as in imagination they have placed themselves in the position of the new comers. After their passage of ten weeks was terminated, and they landed upon Nantasket shore, glad to plant their feet upon that continent which they had chosen as their future home, they tarried for a few days, to recruit from the ill effects attendant upon their long voyage. They now began to look about for a place of habitation. Methinks I see Chickatabot, the chief of the Massachusetts tribe, standing upon this hill and watching the movements of the strange visitors. He had seen, from Squantum Head, the boat which a few days previous had passed up towards Charles River, and now his eagle eye saw another as it leaves the shore and makes a straight wake towards the mouth of his favorite Neponset. He marks them as the ebbing tide sets them towards the North, till they disappear behind Old Hill; they soon re-appear, pass up the quiet waters of Old Harbor, and land upon the south side of Mattapan Neck. He had seen Blackstone at Shawmut, and Walfourd at Mishawan, and hoped that they were to be his nearest pale-faced neighbors. He finds that he is mistaken, and wends his way to his wigwam, at the Massachusetts Fields, to ponder upon these things. As they approached our harbor and marked the landscape as it lay before them, the sloping highlands receding as they approached the shore, and gorgeous with the foliage of early summer, who will wonder at their choice?

A kind word, before I close, to the memory of Capt. Squeb, whose name has been handed down to posterity by our pious progenitor, Roger Clap, as a merciless man, because he landed his passengers at Nantasket. He agreed to bring them to the mouth of Charles River. He called that the mouth, and well might any stranger do so as he approached the coast, and saw the wooded islands apparently closing in on every side, with the great Brewster twice its present size; Nix's Mate, containing twelve acres; Sound Point, a high bluff projecting far towards Long Island Head, with the waters of the Charles, Neponset and Mystick rushing by at every ebb—a channel which no pilot's eye had marked or line had sounded—no warning buoys upon the Centurion nor Upper nor Lower Middle. Well might he call that the mouth of the Charles, and refuse to steer the prow of "that great ship the Mary and John" another fathom up its unknown waters.

I will offer the following sentiment:—

*The Passengers in the Ship "Mary and John"*—Educated by the trials and persecutions of their age, to be the founders of a new country; their posterity meet this day on their sacred hill, and, like Moses from Mt. Pisgah, view the promised land.

The President.—*Ladies and Gentlemen*—It is my duty, as well as my privilege, to acknowledge our obligations to one of our fellow townsmen for the truly liberal and honorable spirit which he has manifested in all the proceedings connected with this celebration. I allude to Col. Enoch Train, who in addition to other acts of munificence, has erected, at his own expense, yonder magnificent flagstaff, from which floats, this day, one of the largest if not *the* largest banner in the world. I therefore propose the following sentiment:—

Health, happiness, and long life to our worthy citizen, Col. Enoch Train. [Great applause.]

Col. TRAIN responded:—

*Mr. President:*

I have taken great pains, I must confess, to erect something substantial. My hope is, that all here present will, for many years to come, on the return of this anniversary, see that staff standing, and those "stripes and stars" floating before the breeze. [Cheers.] We are peculiarly fortunate in our weather to-day, for floating bunting. It was fortunate, I think, that the Declaration of Independence was signed at a favorable season of the year. Had it been the fourth of February, like that cold night when the committee were at your house, Sir, instead of the fourth of July, we could not have been here; we could not have enjoyed the pleasant marches and festivities of this day. [Cheers.]

I observe in this tent some mottoes with complimentary allusions to myself, in one of which Train's Packet Ships are placed in contrast with the ship "Mary and John," which brought the first settlers of our goodly town to these shores. The contrast is truly wonderful between the ships of that day and those of the present; but time will not permit me to enter upon this subject.

Mr. President, I am extremely obliged to this assembly for the cordial manner in which they have received the sentiment with which you have honored me. [Repeated cheers.]

The following sentiment was then announced by the chair:

*The Dorchester Antiquarian and Historical Society*—In treasuring up the memorials of the fathers, it best manifests its regard for posterity. [Cheers.]

EDWARD L. PIERCE, ESQ. being called upon by the President to respond to this sentiment, said:

*Mr. President and Fellow Citizens:*

It was said by that eminent master of social philosophy—Edmund Burke—that people who do not look back to their ancestors, will not look forward to their posterity. Responding for this Society, let me say, that mindful of the generations to come, they turn their reverent eyes to the fathers and founders of this ancient community. Whatever is illustrative of their lives in records, traditions and relics, it gathers into its archives. Thither, in after-times, shall the patriot citizen repair to invigorate his love of country. Thither shall the historian resort, anxious to present to posterity a faithful transcript of our national life. History no longer fulfils her office, when she busies herself only with the movements of armies, the details of politics, the mysteries of cabinets, and the amours of courts. She alone accomplishes her peculiar work, when, walking among the people, the visitant of their homes, the spectator of their amusements, and the student of their customs, ideas and aspirations, she prepares herself to deliver to mankind a luminous chart of human progress. Thus at once is evident, the importance of local historical societies, like the one in whose behalf I now speak.

In collecting the memorials of the fathers, and in celebrating thei virtues as we do to-day, we act well. Their influence is not circumscribed within the narrow limits of the township, where they may have lived and died. It has spread wherever their blood circulates—wherever the genius of their ideas has found its way, on this hemisphere or the other. The whole land is redolent with the perfume of their memories. History bends under the blossoms of their beautiful deeds. So has it ever been with beneficent lives.

The Avon to the Severn runs,
  The Severn to the sea;
And Wickliffe's dust shall spread abroad,
  Wide as the waters be.

[Mr. Pierce closed his speech by eloquently enforcing the importance of maintaining the true spirit of liberty which animated the breasts of our forefathers.]

The President then happily alluded to the valuable services of the Chief Marshal and his assistants, and gave:

*The Chief Marshal of the Day.*—Before his *Flying Artillery* our foes *fly* away, and under his command the "*Ancient*" cannot but be the "*Honorable*" Artillery. [Applause.]

Major Cobb responded as follows:

*Mr. President:*

I am indeed grateful for the flattering sentiment you have just expressed relative to my connection with the volunteer militia of the Commonwealth. I am one of those who believe, with the Constitution of the United States, that "a well-regulated militia is necessary to the security of a free State," and you, Sir, must be undoubtedly aware that in a community like ours, where the military power is expected, in the language of the Constitution of our own State, to be "held in an exact subordination to the civil authority, and be governed by it," that there has been, and it is to be feared there always will be, a dangerous sentiment of contempt entertained by many towards our militia.

Upon these considerations I have thought it my duty to give my countenance and support to our present militia organization. To me, Sir, it seems anything but trifling and contemptible to see citizens, like yourself, distinguished in the callings of civil life, leaving the comforts and quiet of their homes and their places of business, and with a zeal measured only by their love of country, submitting to the rigors of the field and camp, with as little concern for life, and with as much attention to all the details of military discipline, as the trained troops of a standing army, and then quietly returning to the duties of civil life, ready, if need be, to sacrifice home, fortune, even life itself, for their country.

I believe, Sir, there is not enough love of country in the hearts of the people. I believe, too, that a good soldier cannot be otherwise than a good patriot.

I shall therefore, among other things, by precept and example, strive to teach my children the duties of the citizen soldier of the United States of America, believing that by so doing I am inculcating the most enduring lessons of patriotism.

Hoping, Sir, that the duties of the Chief Marshal and his Aids and Assistants have been performed to the acceptance of yourself and the citizens of Dorchester, I will give—

*The Parents of Massachusetts*—Let them *respect* the Volunteer Militia of the Commonwealth as it deserves to be respected, and the service in it cannot be otherwise than *respectable* for their sons. [Applause.]

---

A vote of thanks was then passed to the President, the Secretary, and other officers, the Marshals, the Independent Company of Cadets, the Boston Light Artillery, the choir of Singers. and all who aided in the celebration.

The President announced that the present festivities would be closed by singing the 117th Psalm, to the tune of Old Hundred—a tune in which our fathers delighted to praise the Creator and Preserver of men. The audience then rose and united in singing the following verses:

From all that dwell below the skies,
Let the Creator's praise arise;
Let the Redeemer's name be sung
Through every land, by every tongue.

Eternal are thy mercies, Lord,
Eternal truth attends thy word;
Thy praise shall sound from shore to shore,
Till suns shall rise and set no more.

---

## VOLUNTEER SENTIMENTS.

BY WILLIAM D. SWAN, ESQ.

The Constitution of the United States, and the memory of its immortal defender.

BY CAPT. EBENEZER EATON.

*The Declaration of Independence*—A democratic document, to be read, studied, taught—and always to be remembered, observed and honored.

BY ROBERT VOSE, ESQ.

*The State of New Hampshire*—When asked for her jewels, she can, like the old Roman matron, proudly present to us her sons.

SENT BY HON. WM. FOSTER (AGED 84), OF BOSTON.

*A President—the Man we want*—Not too young for safe counsel, or too old for energetic action; with learning and experience, with independence and courage.

BY NAHUM CAPEN, ESQ.

*The Day we Celebrate.*—What the Sabbath is to the Religious World, this is to the World of Freedom. It brings the nation to every cottage, and the great truths of nationality to every mind. Without its observance the YOUNG cannot be prepared for the practical duties which belong to the citizen, and the OLD would forget the patriotism of their fathers.

BY OLIVER HALL, ESQ.

*The Fourth of July* 1776, *and the Fourth of July* 1855—The former a time of peril, the latter a time of rejoicing.

BY ARTHUR W. AUSTIN, ESQ., WEST ROXBURY.

*Our National Constitution*—Framed by the wisdom and patriotism of our fathers—intrigue may impeach, or traitors may assail it, but the spirit of Washington protects it, the sword of Jackson guards it, and the game blood of the Revolution is able and will defend it forever.

BY AUGUSTUS BROWN, ESQ.

*Old Dorchester.*—After the *Boston Tea Party,* Washington proposed a series of *Free Balls* from Dorchester Heights, music by the *Bunker Hill Band ;* but these *balls* were too democratic, and were declined by a *Dancing Fleet,* which preferred *Bay Water* to *Boston Port.*

BY EDWARD JONES, ESQ.

*The Independence of the United States.*—The fathers who achieved it have gone to their homes. May their posterity, to the latest generations, preserve and protect the precious boon from all ruthless hands, and extend its blessings to "earth's remotest bounds."

FROM THE DORCHESTER ANTIQUARIAN AND HISTORICAL SOCIETY.

*Sons and Daughters of Old Dorchester*—Welcome to your ancestral home. Our meetings on earth will be but few ; but may we all, progenitors and descendants, present and absent, finally be gathered into that temple "not made with hands, eternal in the heavens."

BY A GUEST.

*The Orator of the Day.*—The garlands of literature, of oratory and statesmanship are gracefully wreathed around his honored brow—not the less unfading, not the less immortal, because illumined by a life of patriotism.

BY O. PUTNAM BACON, ESQ.

*The Prayers of a Warham, a Maverick, and a Mather*—They have ascended to heaven ; may they descend in copious showers to bless those institutions —the Church and the School—which their hands planted and their tears watered.

BY R. VOSE, JR., ESQ.

*The President of the United States*—The brave soldier, the accomplished scholar, the true patriot. Intelligence, honesty and fidelity distinguish the administration of every public trust confided to his hands.

# APPENDIX.

---

The following letters constitute a part of the correspondence with the individuals who were invited to be present at the 4th of July Celebration in Dorchester. The replies are, with a few exceptions, addressed to the Committee on Invitations—consisting of Messrs. S. P. Loud, Nahum Capen, Edmund J. Baker, Ebenezer Clapp, Jr., John P. Spooner, Robert Codman, and W. E. Abbott.

---

TO THE CITIZENS OF DORCHESTER, ENGLAND.

*Dorchester, Massachusetts, U. S. A., May* 8, 1855.

The Undersigned, Members of the Dorchester Antiquarian and Historical Society,

To the Citizens of the City of Dorchester, Dorset, Eng.

Friends :—

Your place being the residence of many of our progenitors, and from which this town derived its name, we address you with an affectionate interest. It is comparatively but a few years since our ancestors left their quiet homes and launched forth upon the ocean, to make a new home for themselves and posterity, and take up their abode in this then inhospitable wilderness of savages and wild beasts. As we look back upon the history of this period, it appears as if events had been transpiring for two centuries, to bring forth and educate for the work, this inestimable race of men. They came to worship God according to the dictates of their own consciences ; and although their treatment of those who differed from them in religious sentiment, was often harsh, cruel, and almost inexcusable, yet we must remember that they were the most tolerant of their age, and that toleration was a doctrine not then dreamed of by the great mass of mankind; even now, many are they who fall far short of its christian requirements. We must also admit that it is not just to judge that generation by the standard of the present. We believe that this is almost the only country ever settled, that had not the lower motive of gold, plunder, or conquest, for its paramount object. But time will not permit us to go into a lengthened history of those men; suffice it to say, they loved their native land, sung of its sacred memories, and prayed for its true glory; they had "great contempt of terrestrial distinctions," and felt assured, that "if their names were not found in the register of heralds, they were recorded in the book of life." This state of things continued until they thought that encroachments were made on their chartered rights, which they endeavored to remedy with all the skill of practised diplomatists; but nothing could prevent a final separation; in the fulness of time the breach was made, which might indeed be called "manifest destiny." About thirty-six years after, another little misunderstanding occurred; but the lapse of time has healed all breaches and all misunderstandings, and we claim you as brethren beloved, and recal the time when our fathers sat side by side, gloried in the same country, and looked forward to the same destiny. It was meet that the separation should come, and the great doctrine of "Westward the star of Empire takes its way," be fulfilled. That star has reached its culminating point, and planted its banner by the setting sun; henceforth civilization must travel east, and Asia and Africa be its field of operation.

It is supposed that this town was called Dorchester, on account of the great respect of its early settlers for Rev. John White, a clergyman of your place at that time, and an active instrument in promoting the settlement and procuring its charter. They sailed from Plymouth, England, March 20, and arrived May 30, 1630; they came in the ship Mary and John, Capt. Squeb, and were finally settled down here as a body politic about June 17, 1630. They were reinforced from time to time, and many remained here only for a short period and then went to other places and made new homes. It is estimated that there are now living, in this country, two hundred thousand persons who are descendants of the early settlers of this town.

A little previous to the year 1700 (Oct. 22, 1695), a church was organized in this town, which went to South Carolina and planted another Dorchester; so that in civil affairs you have children and grandchildren in this western world. A large number of persons of the following names, descendants of the early settlers of this town, are now living here or in this vicinity, viz.: Baker, Bird, Blackman, Blake, Bradlee, Billings, Capen, Clapp, Davenport, Foster, Glover, Holmes, Hall, Hawes, Howe, Hewins, Humphreys, Jones, Leeds, Lyon, Moseley, Minot, Pierce, Payson, Preston, Pope, Robinson, Spur, Sumner, Tileston, Tolman, Vose, White, Withington, Wales and Wiswell. Any information concerning these names would be very interesting to us, appreciated, and treasured up for posterity.

The inhabitants of this town propose to celebrate the 79th anniversary of our birth-day as a nation, on the coming July 4th. Hon. Edward Everett, a native of this place, and late Minister Plenipotentiary to Great Britain, will address the assembly. The sons and daughters of the town, wherever scattered, are invited to come to their ancestral home and unite with us on this occasion. It is too much for us to ask that a delegation might be sent from your Borough to add to the interest of this festival; but should one or more of your citizens whom you would approve be in this country, it would give us great pleasure to have them attend as our guests. Dorchester adjoins Boston on the south, contains about 8000 inhabitants, and for its size is one of the wealthiest towns in the country; its valuation last year was $10,182,400. Its location is one of great interest, and its founders had an eye for the beautiful when they pitched their tents upon this land of promise; their hands cultivated these spreading fields and "helped to subdue a wilderness which now blossoms like the rose." Within the last generation science has subdued the elements, and made them applicable to the purposes of man; distance is computed by time and not space, so that you seem neighbors as well as friends, and by this epistle we reach forth across the ocean, offer you the right hand of fellowship, and in imagination look forward to that future when the only question asked by all nations will be, how does it stand related to eternal truth?

With great respect, your Friends,

EDMUND P. TILESTON,
EDMUND J. BAKER,
EBENEZER CLAPP, JR.
WM. D. SWAN,
WM. B. TRASK,
WM. H. RICHARDSON,
JAMES SWAN,
SAMUEL BLAKE,
EDWARD HOLDEN.

---

FROM THE MAYOR OF DORCHESTER, ENG.

TO THE MEMBERS OF THE DORCHESTER ANTIQUARIAN AND HISTORICAL SOCIETY, DORCHESTER, MASSACHUSETTS, U. S.

*South Street, Dorchester, Dorset.* 16*th June*, 1855.

GENTLEMEN AND FRIENDS:—

Your letter, which as Mayor it fell to my lot to receive, has created a feeling of interest amongst us, and we welcome with great cordiality the communication from those whom we may style kinsfolk. I have caused your letter to be printed, and have circulated it amongst such persons especially as are likely to assist us in our inquiries on the subject of it.

I myself, and I believe many others, would gladly pay you a visit, but that we cannot spare the time required to do so.

We feel that we cannot furnish you with an account of our town and neighborhood in such a manner as we would wish, in time for your anniversary, but we hope by the 80th anniversary to be enabled to collect a portfolio for you, which, if you wish, we shall gladly forward to you. I have already a nucleus of the collection.

Mr. White's name is still known in the Borough, and there are still names amongst us which are enumerated by you. The Town itself does not probably exceed, by much, the limits it had when our common ancestors left it.

Being surrounded by the lands of the Duchy of Cornwall, which are held in common, there has been a constant check upon increasing our bounds. We are, however, we trust, increasing our station amongst other towns, and we hope ere long that the obstacle to our extension may be removed.

The County Gaol and other public buildings being situated here, and the Assizes and Quarter Sessions being held here, add to our importance. The suburb of Fordington now forms part of our Borough. We have five Churches, and several Chapels for those whose doctrines differ from the Church of England. Of these churches, two are in Fordington and three in Dorchester. The Holy Trinity Church was rebuilt in 1824—5; the Church of All Saints about five or six years ago. The Church of St. Peters is the oldest church in the town. There is now a scheme on foot for restoring and repairing this church, and for giving greater accommodation to our poorer brethren. When completed, we shall give them upwards of 200 free sittings, and the building will then be a handsome specimen of architecture. At present the committee are stayed by want of sufficient funds.

Two important Railways, the London and South Western and the Great Western, approach us, whilst at eight miles distance we have the Port of Weymouth, and the Island of Portland, with the Quarries, whereon the Government have established Convict Prisons, and by convict labor in great part they are forming a breakwater.

Our design is to furnish you, if acceptable, with a full description of the town and neighborhood, accompanied by such views as we may be able to procure or furnish to illustrate our account. We do not think we can do this with justice to the subject before next summer, but if you will then accept it as a pledge of good feeling and good fellowship, it is humbly at your service.

You will perhaps let me know how these matters should be sent to you; and with every good wish for your welfare,

I remain yours very faithfully,

THOS. COOMBS, *Mayor.*

---

FROM THE MIDWAY SOCIETY, GEORGIA.

RICEBORO', LIBERTY Co., Ga., June 4th, 1855.

*Gentlemen:*

Your letter dated Dorchester, Mass., May 11th, 1855, has been received by the Midway Society. You mention that in the year 1695 (Oct. 22) "a church was formed in this town, which went to South Carolina and settled in a place which they called Dorchester," and "subsequently they removed to Midway, in Georgia;" and you also inquire, "whether any of the descendants of those who went off from this town are now living." In reply, we would state that your communication was received with much pleasure. It recalled to our minds the ties of consanguinity, and those traditional associations, which have ever endeared in our memories the home of our ancestors. We are happy to inform you that, according to our records, the church organized in Dorchester, Mass., in the year 1695, A. D., of which the Rev. Joseph Lord was pastor, settled in Dorchester and Beach Hill, S. C., during the same year, and continued there until the year 1752—a period of fifty-seven years, when the Society being in want of lands for the settlement of their children, began to remove to Midway, in Georgia, and located there upon the 6th of December, 1752, where most of their descendants remain until the present time. About one half of the present population of Liberty County are related to these settlers. Others have followed the westward tide of emigration. During the infancy of the church at Midway, our society was much afflicted with disease, annoyed by the predatory incursions of Indians, and sacked by the rapacious British during our struggle for Independence. During the continuance of the war, our society was much scattered, but with the news of peace a brighter day dawned. Our church and society was then settled upon a sure and solid basis, and, we hope, has proved a blessing to very many of our race.

The mission upon which this church and society left Dorchester, was to "encourage the settlement of churches, and the promotion of religion in the Southern plantations." We trust this mission has been a successful one. Many, heralds of the cross, have gone forth from our society to preach the Gospel; some to China and Burmah, some to our sister States, whilst others have chosen our colored population as their field of usefulness. We have not been altogether forgetful of our origin. In the year 1795, a sermon was preached by the Rev. Cyrus Gildersleeve, pastor of Midway Church at that time, commemorative of the one hundredth anniversary of our society since its formation in Dorchester, Mass. The church and society at Midway (which has preserved its Congregationalism intact to the present time) also celebrated on the 4th, 5th and 6th of December, 1852, the centennial anniversary of our settlement here. Our exercises were commenced by a sermon from the Rev. J. S. R. Axson (who had been our pastor for seventeen years, now President of Greensboro', Geo., Female College), a man of sterling piety, rare intelligence, and polished eloquence. On the next day, Prof. John B. Mallard read an essay, containing an epitome of all the historical associations connected with our early settlement. On the 6th, Judge William Law delivered an oration on the character, objects and influences of our church and society.

Thus we have endeavored to refresh our memories with the history of the past, and impress them upon the minds of our children.

The descendants of the fathers of our society assembled from many remote

19

points, and participated with us in the festivities of that occasion. We regret that we were so remiss in our duty, as not to have extended an invitation to you to unite with us.

We feared that sad changes of time had obliterated us from the memory of our Northern relatives and friends; but now that you have sought us out, to renew our acquaintance, your kindness will render you doubly dear to us. * * * We are pleased to infer, from your invitation to unite with you in the celebration of the ensuing 4th of July, that a sentiment of nationality still pervades our ancestral town.

* * * * * * * * * * *

In your letter you say, "We give you our fraternal greeting, and through you, your Society, wishing you peace, prosperity and every Christian grace." Most willingly do we accept these proffers of love and friendship, and tender you our reciprocity of sentiment. The names of Dorchester and Plymouth are dear to us. The Puritans of New England have impressed their character upon America. Our ancestors at Midway, bringing with them a love of religion, liberty and law, were the first in Georgia to declare in favor of independence, and the name of Liberty County has been given to our former parish in testimony of the fact. The descendants of the original settlers of Midway have spread themselves over Georgia, and the Southern States, as the pioneers of religion, education and jurisprudence. Our Society at present occupies a commanding position upon the seaboard of Georgia. Considerable progress has been made in civil and religious development, agricultural science, wealth and population. We beg leave to refer you, for further particulars, to White's Historical Collections of Georgia, as containing a full and authentic statement of our Society, which might interest some of our Northern friends. We will mention, also, that within about seven miles of Midway Church, we have a neat village, called Dorchester, in honor of our ancestral town, whose citizens are noted for their intelligence and hospitality. Our present pastors are the Rev. D. L. Buttolph, of New York, and the Rev. John F. Baker, of Wilkesbarre, Pa.

The undersigned have been appointed a committee of correspondence, and we have endeavored to respond to your communication, detailing some matters of interest. We have appointed a delegation of Messrs. G. W. Walthour, John B. Barnard, and Samuel M. Varnadoe, to attend your celebration, and we would be glad for you to receive them in the name of the Midway Society.

Please accept our thanks for your hospitable invitation, fraternal feelings, and cordial greetings.

May we be ever united in the bonds of patriotism and Christian love, and be mutually remembered at a throne of grace.

Yours most truly,

W. S. Norman,
S. M. Varnadoe,
A. Winn,
W. S. Baker,
John B. Barnard, } *Cor. Com.*

FROM HON. ROBERT C. WINTHROP.

NEWPORT, R. I., 3d July, 1855.

*Gentlemen :*

Unexpected and unavoidable absence from home will deprive me of the pleasure of fulfilling my engagement to be present at the Dorchester Festival to-morrow. I regret extremely to lose the Oration of my distinguished friend, Mr. Everett, and to miss the opportunity of meeting the sons and daughters of Dorchester on so interesting an occasion.

I cannot altogether forget that I have some claim to be among them, apart from the complimentary invitation with which I have been honored. In your good old Town have lived, in years past, not a few of those with whom I have been connected by the nearest ties both of affection and of blood. The vote of Dorchester in favor of the adoption of the Constitution of the United States—the most important vote she was ever called upon to cast—was given by the hand of my near maternal relative, James Bowdoin, whose name has been fitly assigned to one of the beautiful hills within your borders. Not a few of the pleasantest hours of my boyhood were passed upon that hill; and, certainly, there is no prospect which I have ever seen since, either at home or abroad, which has left a more vivid impression on my mind for variety and beauty, than that of my native city, with its charming environs and lovely harbor, as viewed from the old summer house which has but recently disappeared from Mount Bowdoin.

It would have afforded me real pleasure to unite with you in recalling the interesting events of your early history, and in renewing our common pledges of fidelity and devotion to the Independence, the Constitution, and the Union of our Country. But it is only in my power to thank you once more for your obliging invitation, and to offer to the people of Dorchester my cordial wishes both for the success of the occasion, and for their continued prosperity and welfare. Believe me, dear sir,

Very sincerely and faithfully,

Your Friend and Servant,

ROB'T C. WINTHROP.

---

FROM HON. RUFUS CHOATE.

BOSTON, July 3d, 1855.

*Gentlemen :*

I have delayed a formal reply to your kind invitation for the 4th instant, in the hope that I might be well enough to accept it; yet apprehensive that I should not. My recovery, though advancing, is yet so incomplete that, as I feared, it is now certain I shall not have the pleasure of sharing in all that entertainment to which the taste and public spirit of Dorchester are sure to give so much attraction.

The discourse of Mr. Everett, I cannot deny myself the gratification and instruction of attending. If it were only to see and hear the consummate orator, returning from so many triumphs of eloquence, to speak on the sublime themes of Independence and Union, among the graves of home, and to the children of his father's friends, and in sight of the ridges of the great war, still unobliterated, on his native heights—if it were only to see and hear genius, erudition and practice unequalled under stimulations and with advantages so unwonted, the temptation would be enough. But the moderate and healing counsels of a good, wise, and great man, capacious of his whole country, are matter even more attractive; and to listen to these chiefly I would be, and wish all could be, of his audience.

I am with great regard, Your obedient servant,

RUFUS CHOATE.

---

Mr. Choate gave further expression to his feelings through the columns of the Boston Courier, in the article which follows.

"Mr. Everett at Home.—The newspapers will have, before this time, placed Mr. Everett's admirable discourse in the hands of the whole public; but one of his audience may still be permitted to speak of the impression it made on him in the actual delivery. It is little to say that it had brilliant success. Certainly it had. Some five or six thousand persons—but, however, a vast multitude—ladies and gentlemen, children in green chaplets from school, and old age with his staff shaking in both his hands; of all varieties of culture and of opinion—by silence, by tears, by laughter, by hearty and frequent applause, for more than two hours of not very comfortable weather, confessed the spell of the spoken eloquence of written thoughts and thoughts not written; and when he ended, sat still fixed to hear, as if the spell would not be broken.

"It is saying more to say that it deserved all its success. The noble, affluent and beautiful genius, and the effective trained and popular talent, all remain at their best. The same playfulness, the same elegance, the same memory of his learning, the same justness and exactness of thought and image, the same discernment of truth, the same fidelity to history and biography, the same philosophic grasp and sweep, the same intense American feeling; occasionally an ascent to more than his former height of eloquence, pathos and poetry—an impression altogether of more and even truer wealth of mind. One is glad to see such powers and such attainments bearing a charmed life. Long and late be the day when the 'old bell' shall announce that the charm is dissolved, and the life on earth is quenched.

"The topics and method of the discourse, now that it is printed, we need not dwell on. The treatment of the whole subject, too, can be appreciated by those who did not hear him, only by reading it. What struck us, among other things was, the affectionate and pains-taking fidelity with which the local history and biography of Dorchester were displayed — its periods, growth, acts, and good men in church and state remembered as if it were a duty of justice and genealogy as well as love—and yet that all these narrower annals were so gracefully connected with, and made to exemplify a history of heroic times, and renowned events—'the foundation of a state'—the maxims and arts imperial by which it lives, grows, and works out its ends —the throes and glory of revolution—effected by the shedding of the blood of man, and conducting to a true national life. In this way Dorchester became representative, and as it were illustrious—as a handful of minerals may be made to show forth the history of a world, and of cycles.

"More than once the speaker rose from the plane of his elegant and clear English, and moving narrative, and just thought, to passages of superlative beauty. Of these were that which sketched the last man of the Massachusetts tribe of Indians; that which contrasted the loving, cultivated, and auxiliar nature which enfolds us, with that austerer nature which repelled the first settlers; that which imagined the Titan sleep of the spent wave at Nahant; that which condensed the long wrongs of the colonial period into the image of a slow 'night, swept away by the first sharp volley on Lexington green;' and, above all, that which conceived the memories and the anticipations that might labor in the 'soul of Washington, at that decisive hour, as he stood upon the heights of Dorchester, with the holy stars for his camp-fire, and the deep folding shadows of night, looped by the hand of God, to the four quarters of the sky, for the curtains of his tent.'

"And these all, in their places, were appropriate, spontaneous, and helpful. *Nunc erat his locus.*

"Shall we confess that there was a certain trait pervading the whole discourse, which gave it an interest even beyond its wisdom and eloquence? More than ever before, in our observations of his public efforts, his heart was allowed to flow from his lips. It was, as when one of a large and happy household, on a holiday, remembers and recalls to the rest the time when the oldest of them were young—what they used to see, and what they used to hear told—the speaker and the hearer the while, sometimes smiling and sometimes sad—smiling often with a tear in the eye. Such he seemed, and those who have only seen and heard him on some high theme and day, and when he might appear to be pleading for the crown of gold, should have seen and heard him *at home*, to know and feel how much he is made to be loved.

"Mr. Everett declares himself 'retired from public life, without the expectation or the wish to return to it, but the contrary, and that few things would better please him than to find a quiet retreat in his native town, where he may pass the rest of his humble career in the serious studies and tranquil pursuits which befit the decline of life, till the same old bell shall announce that the chequered scene is over, and the weary is at rest.' Scholars will recall the pathetic expression of Cicero: *Nunc vero, quoniam, quae patavi esse preclara, expertus sum, quam essent inania, cum omnibus Musis rationem habere cogito.* But this was after his splendid consulship, and when he had no longer a civil future. Until that has been Mr. Everett's whole experience, why should he employ his language?"

FROM THE MAYOR OF THE CITY OF BOSTON.

MAYOR'S OFFICE, CITY HALL, Boston, June 21st, 1855.

*Gentlemen:*

A celebration of the political birth-day of the nation in Boston, will necessarily prevent me from participating in similar festivities abroad. The beautiful place where the distinguished orator and statesman who officiates on the occasion of your celebration, and the Governor of the Commonwealth, were born, possesses rare advantages for giving interest to the gathering.

From the intimate relationship existing between Dorchester and Boston; their historical associations, their united efforts in the first settlement of New England and in the revolutionary struggle through which they passed, there is no reason for supposing that a friendship thus established, will ever decline, while business intercourse and the refinements of social life are the accompaniments of christian civilization.

Very respectfully, I have the honor to remain,

Your obedient servant,

J. V. C. SMITH.

*Dorchester and Boston.*—As they were in youth, so may they remain in age — friends and associates, giving their influence for the advancement of society and the security of the privileges, good institutions and liberties of our common country.

---

FROM HON. DAVID SEARS, OF BOSTON.

BEACON STREET, BOSTON, June 23d, 1855.

*Gentlemen:*

I regret that I cannot do myself the honor to accept the invitation of the Citizens of Dorchester, without distinction of party, to celebrate the 4th of July next, in a manner suited to the great birth-day of freedom. But an engagement to dine with the Massachusetts Society of the Cincinnati, puts it out of my power.

The relations between Boston and Dorchester have always been those of friendship and courtesy, founded on a feeling of mutual respect, and cemented by many acts of sympathy and kindness.

Boston can never forget the day when her citizens looked with an anxious eye to the heights of Dorchester for relief, nor can she cease to remember that to the gallant array of freemen assembled there for action on the night of the 4th of March, 1776, she was saved from disgrace, and enabled to resume that high position among the sons of enlightened freedom which it has ever since been her endeavor to maintain.

The influence of Dorchester extends far beyond her limits. Her children are well known and esteemed, and every where show evidence of the soundness of their principles, and the excellence of their education. None more so than the Hon. Edward Everett, whom you have invited to address you on the coming national anniversary. His name is already historical, and he adds and gives back honor to his birth-place. I have known him since boyhood, followed his course with interest, from his first labors for distinction, to his masterly efforts for his country's good in the Department of State, and in every position, and under all circumstances, he has shone forth — the scholar, the statesman, and the gentleman.

With great consideration, and very respectfully,

Your obedient servant,

DAVID SEARS.

---

FROM HON. S. D. BRADFORD.

West Roxbury, 28th June, 1855.

*Gentlemen :*

I have received your much respected favor inviting me to join the citizens of Dorchester in celebrating the 4th of July, "in a manner suited to the great birth-day of freedom, and without distinction of party."

I thank you for this proof of your remembrance and regard, and regret that a prior engagement beyond my control will prevent my being present upon the occasion indicated, which offers so many inducements to every lover of freedom and his country.

I congratulate you that the county of Norfolk and the town of Dorchester can number amongst its sons so distinguished a statesman and such a profound scholar and orator as the Hon. Edward Everett, and that he is to deliver the oration in the presence of the inhabitants of his native place and of the towns in the vicinity, and also that a deputation may be expected from the flourishing colony in Georgia planted by Dorchester so may years ago, which cannot fail to add greatly to the attractions of the day.

You have said that it will be celebrated "without distinction of party," which reminds me of the earlier days of our Republic, when in every town there might be found *Democrats* and *Federalists,* the apologists of all the wrongs done us by France and Great Britain, but *not one American,* who felt that true patriotism always rises above party, is never confined by geographical boundaries, and embraces the whole country, East, West, North and South.

That amongst our countrymen, who had so recently fought and triumphed together, there should have been such divisions in celebrating the birth-day of our national freedom, would seem almost incredible, were it not recorded in history, besides being remembered by many now living.

That illustrious patriot General Jackson, in speaking of Columbus, once called him "the firm, daring, lofty spirit who gave a continent to civilization and liberty a land to abide in ;" and who can look now upon this beautiful and highly favored land, in its present state of prosperity and greatness, without feeling what a debt of gratitude we owe to Washington and the founders of our Republic for having defended the country discovered by Columbus; and also how essential it is to guard and preserve *the Union* of these States, without which we could no longer be prosperous or great?

Let us never forget, then, the words of the Father of his country, "that there will always be reason to distrust the patriotism of those, who in any quarter may endeavor to weaken its bands;" and let us all (whatever may be our political preferences) resolve "that the Constitution, the object of our reverence, the bond of our Union, our defence in danger, the source of our prosperity in peace, shall descend, as we have received it, uncorrupted by sophistical construction, to the latest posterity."

Believe me to remain, with sentiments of great respect,

Your most obedient servant,

S. D. BRADFORD.

---

FROM HON. JULIUS ROCKWELL.

PITTSFIELD, July 22, 1855.

*Gentlemen:*

I have this day received your kind invitation to attend the celebration of the Anniversary of Independence at Dorchester, on the 4th of July. Previous to my knowledge that this anniversary was to be celebrated at Dorchester, under circumstances of so great interest, I had engaged to preside at a celebration in this town, by the people of the county. This engagement I must fulfil, and it well prevent my attending at Dorchester. Otherwise I would have most gladly availed myself of the opportunity to attend your celebration.

William Rockwell, my ancestor, was one of the original, or early settlers of that town, and I believe he was a worthy and useful man. The genealogy has been traced out by members of my family, with great interest and satisfaction; and I have taken care to preserve such historical evidences as I have been able to obtain.

I need hardly say, that nothing of this kind could be so interesting to me as this celebration. I have seen the good town of Dorchester, and am aware of its present honorable position among the towns of our beloved commonwealth. But when I visited that town, I was not aware of the fact so interesting to me, that my blood was drawn from a heart which found freedom and the liberty of conscience there. If my life is spared, it will be deemed by me a sacred duty to point out to my children the spot where that heart first realized the Christian liberty for which it made so many sacrifices, and endured so great labor and privation; in the hope that they may preserve the principles and emulate the virtues which were there sustained and exhibited.

With great respect, your obedient servant,

JULIUS ROCKWELL.

FROM REV. W. A. STEARNS, D. D.

AMHERST COLLEGE, 29th June, 1855.

*Gentlemen:*

Your favor of May 10th, giving me an invitation to attend your proposed celebration of the 4th of July, and "to participate in its festivities," was duly received. I put off sending the appropriate acknowledgment, as I was not without hope that by a little delay I might respond to your politeness with an affirmative answer. But circumstances, the most imperious of which is sickness in my family, will prevent me from enjoying the pleasure of being with you on that interesting occasion. I regret this deeply, as the town of Dorchester has always been vividly associated, in my mind, with the noble struggles and triumphs of our fathers for liberty. "Dorchester heights" is among the magic words which quicken the blood of every American, when he reads the history of his native land. But great as this honor may be, the town is no less favored, by being the birth-place of that most distinguished statesman who has consented to adorn the celebration with an address. Whether as a dignitary of the Senate of the United States, or as Governor of his native Commonwealth; as representing his country at the proudest of the European courts, or as filling the chair of Webster in the office of Secretary of State; as presiding over the interests of science and letters in our venerated University; as moving in the humble walks of a private citizen, or as stirring the people with his enchanting eloquence, *his* eminences are in no respect surpassed by those which have made your town immortal in the history of our revolution.

Gentlemen, as I cannot be with you on the interesting occasion anticipated, permit me to embody my feelings in a brief sentiment:

*Dorchester and her distinguished Son*—The "heights" of both will forever be remembered as heights of glory in the history of our country.

I am, gentlemen, most respectfully,

Your obedient servant,

W. A. STEARNS.

---

FROM HON. SAMUEL BRECK.

PHILADELPHIA, June 4th, 1855.

*Gentlemen:*

I gratefully acknowledge the receipt of an invitation to a dinner in celebration of the 4th of July next, by the citizens of Dorchester. And as this year is the 225th anniversary of the settlement of that town, its sons and daughters, wherever residing, are called together, to partake of the festival to be given that day, in honor of our National Independence.

I would seize with eagerness this opportunity to visit the resting place of my remote American ancestors, did not my advanced age of eighty-four years prevent me. In Dorchester are the graves of my progenitor, Edward Breck, and several of his children. He was selectman of that town for five years, from 1641 and following, and is the honored root from whom sprang a numerous progeny, now scattered from sea to sea; and, generally, bearing our name in good repute, and sometimes with considerable distinction, in the law, the pulpit, and in medicine.

Unsuited, then, for the convivial board, I am most reluctantly obliged to deny myself the pleasure and honor I should receive were I able to wait upon you.

The oration of Mr. Everett — a man so eloquent, so eminent in every accomplishment of mind and heart — would of itself be a sufficient attraction, were not the leaden weight of old age in my heels. Should opportunity offer, I pray you to assure him of my highest esteem and respect. Please, sir, to accept for yourself and the gentlemen associated with you, the assurance of cordial thanks and great respect.

SAMUEL BRECK.

---

FROM REV. LEONARD WITHINGTON.

NEWBURY, June 30th, 1855.

*Gentlemen :*

I suppose it is almost superfluous to write, as I imagine our letters crossed each other on the way. There was a little delay in yours, from mis-direction. I have already sent one which I suppose you have received, in which I say it will be impossible for me to be at Dorchester on the 4th, which I regret. The attractions are great. I ventured in my last to communicate a sentiment — something like this :

*Old Dorchester* — She welcomes to her maternal bosom this day her original and her adopted sons ; her eye sees that they are *many*, her heart feels that they are *one*.

Mr. Everett, I have no doubt, will equal the high expectations his name must raise.

With respect, yours,

L. WITHINGTON.

---

FROM HON. JUDGE DEWEY.

NORTHAMPTON, June 20th, 1855.

*Gentlemen :*

It would give me great pleasure to accept the invitation of the Committee of the Citizens of Dorchester, "to unite with them in celebrating the 4th of July next, in a manner suited to the great birth-day of freedom," but indispensable engagements elsewhere will render it impracticable. I am happy to be remembered by you as one of the descendants of the ancient town of

Dorchester, that having been the residence of Thomas Dewey, my first ancestor from England, at the early period of 1634, and from whom I am the fifth generation in descent. I shall ever delight to recognize my relation to old Dorchester, honored as she is by being probably the earliest place in Massachusetts, entered upon by civilized men, — rich as she is in her incidents and memorials appertaining to the days of our revolutionary struggles, — and blessed with a present generation who know how to appreciate the blessings of civil and religious liberty.

Accept the assurances of my highest respect.

Your obedient servant,

CHARLES A. DEWEY.

---

FROM FLAVEL MOSELEY, ESQ.

CHICAGO, ILL., June 8th, 1855.

*Gentlemen:*

I feel very much gratified, as well as highly honored, with your polite invitation to be present on the 4th of July next, and participate with you in the festivities of the "great birth-day of freedom."

There is no place, in the wide world, whose citizens I would more gladly meet, than those of the good old town of Dorchester. The very *name* of your town awakens in my mind pleasing memories of the past. Dorchester was the birth-place of my ancestors. The name was familiar to my childhood. I am a stranger to most of the people of your place; but not to the place itself. The first time I ever visited Massachusetts, I hastened to Dorchester; and without a personal acquaintance with a single individual there, I spent happy hours, viewing and admiring its beautiful scenery; yet loving it still more, for its historic associations.

My regret, that I cannot be present at your celebration, is increased by the consideration that I shall miss the opportunity of listening to the eloquence of him who is to address you on the occasion.

I am, gentlemen, with much respect,

Your obedient servant,

FLAVEL MOSELEY.

---

FROM HON. JUDGE LANE.

SANDUSKY, OHIO, May 29th, 1855.

*Gentlemen:*

It is among the most valued treasures of my memory, that I am descended from one, who was numbered with the inhabitants of Dorchester more than two hundred years ago. I have therefore received, with lively pleasure, an invitation to share in your celebration of the 4th of July. If I can command time and opportunity, I shall most willingly welcome the occasion. Meanwhile it is no slight gratification that the children of Mattapan are willing to name me among their brethren.

I am, with much consideration,

E. LANE.

---

FROM W. W. MATHER, ESQ.

COLUMBUS, OHIO, July 2d, 1855.

*Gentlemen :*

Your kind letter of invitation to attend the celebration of "the birth-day of freedom," and to participate in the festivities of the day at Dorchester, was received on my return from the East. I have been spending some weeks at West Point, as one of the board of visitors attending the examination of the Cadets of the United States Military Academy.

I would gladly have availed myself of this opportunity to have visited Dorchester, had I known it earlier. It would have been very pleasant to visit Dorchester, Boston and Cambridge, the scenes of active usefulness of my ancestors, Richard and Increase Mather, and join in the festivities with other descendants of the early settlers of New England, in commemorating a nation's birth-day — to see their faces, and hear the sentiments flow from their lips on such an occasion.

I regret that I cannot avail myself of this opportunity.

Please accept the kindest regards and best wishes of,

Your obedient servant,

W. W. MATHER.

---

FROM A. M. CLAPP, ESQ.

BUFFALO, June 21st, 1855.

*Gentlemen :*

I have the honor to acknowledge your kind invitation to participate in the festivities of the coming anniversary of our National Independence, with the citizens of Dorchester. I regret exceedingly that other engagements will prevent my being present with you on that occasion. I am proud to be recognized as a descendant of the early settlers of Dorchester, and it would afford me unalloyed satisfaction to mingle with the friends and descendants of my ancestors on the very soil where they sustained good lives and upright characters, and exemplified the principles of true philanthropy and justice as private citizens or public servants, and to commemorate with you their deeds of valor and philanthropy. I look to Boston and its vicinage with profound respect and veneration, as the Athens of this hemisphere, whose broad light of religion and knowledge has illumined a great nation, extending from Pilgrim Rock to the golden sands of the Pacific. Yours is classic soil. It is the birth-place of American liberty, whose infant hours were spent in Faneuil Hall, and whose baptism was performed in the purest blood of New England, on the very soil you tread in commemorating its triumph over every foe.

* * * * * * * *

It would be pleasant to join with you on this occasion. It would be delightful to mingle with those who have succeeded to the manors of our ancestors, and shared the blessings of New England life in its full fruition, while the more adventurous of our stock have plunged into the forests of the West, and by the hard hand of industry have made them to "bud and blossom as the rose." While we have enjoyed less of the world than you who have been cradled where your ancestors were graved, and who will be graved near the spot where your progeny are cradled, we have seen more of its rugged paths and privations. Thus we have each and all borne our parts in the drama of life, each impressed with the belief that the true honor of man lies in acting well the part allotted to him.

With much respect, yours, &c.

A. M. CLAPP.

---

FROM OLIVER FROST, ESQ.

BOSTON, June 22d, 1855.

*Gentlemen:*

It is with no ordinary pleasure that I acknowledge the receipt of your very polite invitation to meet "the citizens of Dorchester without distinction of party," on the 4th of July next, and to participate in the festivities of the day.

Nothing but some unforeseen contingency shall prevent me from embracing the opportunity for the enjoyment of the rich intellectual feast which awaits you from your distinguished orator, as well as the other festivities of the occasion.

The day you celebrate is the anniversary of our country's freedom, the birth-day of independence to America, however bounded; its events, the seminal of the freedom of the world. It is a day worthy of commemoration through all time, and has been aptly called our political Sabbath. And it is a cheering reflection to all good citizens, that every passing year brings one day in its calendar, when twenty millions of freemen are content to cease from party strife, and unite upon one common platform at the shrine of patriotism. No surer guaranty for the perpetuity of the Union, or for its rescue from all external or internal attempts to weaken its bonds, need be desired than such demonstrations as your public-spirited people have determined upon. A community combining all classes, from the most refined intellect, abundantly enriched with classic lore and modern learning, to the most humble artisan; from the independent lord of the manor, to the toiling gardener; from the merchant prince to his stevedore, have agreed to unite in doing honor to the brave men, who had the moral courage to tell the proudest nation on the earth, that henceforth we ought to be and will be free—to commemorate the day in renewed pledges to each other, that the sacred charter of our liberties shall not be dishonored, but transmitted unsullied to our children. These are the fortresses that shall bid defiance to all who may attempt to invade our liberties.

In conclusion, allow me to offer, on the occasion, the following sentiment, in case of absence:

*Dorchester* — She has been shorn of her *Heights* and her *Washington*. Her only reclamation must be the annexation of the Athens of America to her dominions.

I have the honor to be, gentlemen,

With sentiments of the highest respect,

Your obedient servant,

OLIVER FROST.

---

FROM JOSEPH BRECK, ESQ.

BOSTON, July 2d, 1855.

*Gentlemen:*

It would give me great pleasure to attend the 225th anniversary of the settlement of Dorchester, but other engagements will prevent me.

All my ancestors in a direct line, except my father, died and were buried in Dorchester. I am the third son of Jonathan, who was the oldest son of Edward, who was the oldest son of Edward, who was the oldest son of Ensign Edward, who was the oldest son of Capt. John, who was the oldest son of Edward Breck, who came from Ashton, England, in 1630, and settled in Dorchester the same year; was member of the church in 1636; freeman, 1639; one of the selectmen in years 1642, 46, 55, 56, 59; was one of a committee to build a meeting-house in 1645, and died in the year 1662. His son Capt. John was a man of great energy of character, and great grandfather to the Hon. Samuel Breck, now living in Philadelphia, at the advanced age of 84. Many of the descendants are men of sterling character, inheriting the sound moral principles of their ancestors.

The Hon. S. P. Loud now occupies the homestead of my ancestors. He married a great grand-daughter of Ensign Edward Breck, and grand-daughter of the honored James Robinson, now many years deceased.

As my elder brother is deceased, and the next in age at a distance, I represent the oldest son, in direct succession, of one of the worthy settlers of your ancient town.

Permit me, therefore, to give the following sentiment:

*The Descendants of the worthy Settlers of Dorchester* — Scattered throughout the length and breadth of the land. May they ever bear in mind the moral worth and high religious principles of their honored ancestors, and in their lives carry out their design of establishing a free country, where every man should have the privilege of worshipping God agreeably to the dictates of his own conscience.

Respectfully yours,

JOSEPH BRECK.

---

FROM GEN. WILLIAM H. SUMNER.

JAMAICA PLAIN, July 3d, 1855.

*Gentlemen:*

You did me the favor to invite me to participate in the festivities of the 4th of July, in Dorchester.

How delighted should I be, were it prudent that I should expose myself by going into a crowd, to hear the discourse of that great orator, Edward Everett, of whose nativity Dorchester may well be proud. He will doubtless give you the early history of Mattapan, and will probably relate to you (if he has time for such details) an instance recorded by Winthrop, of the "wonderful working of a kind Providence," in relation to the preservation of the first meeting-house, and the life of Rev. Mr. Maverick, who had charge of it, on the explosion of some gunpowder which he was drying in the building.

* * * * * * * * * *

If it were consistent with the dignity of this occasion, I could relate to you many circumstances which give me an unusual interest in this celebration. Some of these are minute, and relate to localities of individuals. But if these are not divulged upon occasions like the present, when the ears of all the renowned collectors of the Annals of Dorchester are open, is there not danger, if they are of any value, that they will pass off with the fleeting breath of those who could now narrate them? How complete would be the history of Dorchester, if the events, both great and small, which are in the memory of all those who are present, were collected! For myself, being in the habit of dealing in small things, I will contribute an item or two towards making it so, if you will excuse the egotism which will be necessary for their recital.

Although Roxbury was the place of my nativity, yet during my minority, in the latter end of the last century, I became possessed of a paternal estate on the boundaries of Dorchester, which has obtained great celebrity by the scientific cultivation of its present owner, the distinguished gentleman who presides at your festival. Upon a part of this, I resided, for many happy years, and am thus permitted, through associations of a most interesting nature, to indulge in all the feelings of a present townsman.

One of these circumstances is, that I am now the owner, by will, or inheritance, from my ancestors, of all or a part of several pieces of land in the town, which have been held in the family for upwards of a century. One of these, containing forty-one acres, was conveyed to my great-grandfather, Edward Sumner, and my grandfather, Increase Sumner, by Ralph Morgan, in the year 1742. Another, by Samuel Leeds, of seven acres of upland and the marsh round about it, called Leeds's Neck, to my grandfather, Increase Sumner, in 1747; and another, of three acres of fresh meadow, which was conveyed by Jerijah Wales in 1743.

Some of the orator's audience, though *he* may not, will remember the opening of the road in 1808, across the second piece above described. This, at the time, was no small undertaking. It was commenced by the gratuitous grant of the lands of Newell & Niles, the owners of Commercial Point, on the one side of the Mill Creek, and myself, the owner of Leeds's Neck, on the other. Although this is a great improvement, as it now appears, yet it is, like many other things, less in its accomplishment than in its design. The original plan was to build a solid dam, instead of a bridge, across Mill Creek, and for this purpose an act of incorporation was obtained, and a company formed,* entitled the "Dorchester Mill Corporation." To the failure of the original project may be attributed the comparative stillness of these two points of land, which, from the depth of water bordering them, are as favorably situated for external navigation as for manufacturing purposes.

I take some pride, as an agriculturist, in having introduced into Dorchester, upon my marsh at Leeds's Neck, the mode of ditching which is now universally adopted; ditches, one rod apart from each other, of the width of a spade, three and a half feet deep at the lower end, next the creek, and two

---

* It was authorized to "build a Dam from Commercial Point, across Mill Creek, to Leeds's Neck," thus affording "seats for a number of Mills to carry on various manufactories." The principal obstacle was the grist mill above; to obviate this, Newell & Niles, in behalf of themselves and their associates, agreed with Thomas and Ebenezer D. Tileston, owners of the Mill, to transfer their rights to the Company, upon condition that it would build them "a new Mill," of equal power, "on the contemplated dam." The expense of the proposed dam, including the highway to be opened from the Neponset road to Commercial Point, was estimated at ten thousand dollars, which was to be divided into one hundred shares. Seventy-seven of these were taken up, by forty-one individuals; but the Messrs. Tilestons receding from the offer, the whole project was defeated, and a bridge, instead of a dam, was constructed, as a necessary consequence. This bridge soon after went to destruction, although the proprietors contributed largely to its maintenance; but it did not obtain its present eligible condition, until it was assumed by the town.

The following are the names of the forty-one individuals referred to:—Newell, Niles & Co., 20 shares; William H. Sumner, 8; James Ivers, 5; Mrs. Saunders and Miss Beach, 3; Edward Preston, Ebenezer Weld, John F. Pierce, Edward Holden, Thomas Tileston, Edward Robinson, Amasa Stetson, 2 each; Ezekiel Burley, Andrew Thayer, Daniel Withington, Adam Perry, John Kelton, Cyrus Balkcom, Frederic and William Pope, James Humphries, Joseph Clap, Samuel Withington, Samuel Withington, Jr., Ebenezer Clap, Jonathan Pierce, Jr., George Minot, Isaac Clapp, John Holden, Samuel Payson, Nathaniel Clapp, Ebenezer Adams, ——— Cloflen, Phinehas Holden, Edward Sharp, Jonathan Rawson, Benjamin Fuller, Abner Gardner, 1 each; Talbot & Swan, 1.

and a half feet at the upper end, towards the shore, instead of two or three feet wide as practised at that time. This mode of ditching, so far as I am informed, was introduced by Nathaniel Adams, Esq., of Medford, upon "the Royal farm," which was partly owned by myself. Having there seen the success which attended it upon a lot of coarse marsh, of ninety acres (which lie between the Middlesex Canal and the Medford Turnpike), by bringing in black grass and other seeded grasses of two and a half tons to the acre, and some parts of which were mowed twice in a season, I engaged Mr. Hall, a Medford ditcher, to come over to Dorchester and treat my marsh in a like manner. He had been at work but a few days, and made several piles of sods from the ditches he had dug, and as I was standing by him while he was at work, Gov. Robbins hailed me, from the road, and asked what I was about, digging my marsh all into sods? I explained to him the benefits which had resulted from this mode of ditching upon the Royal farm, and of which Mr. Hall was a witness, when he became so convinced of its superiority that he engaged Mr. Hall, at once, to work for him, after he had done with me.

My residence in Dorchester was interesting, particularly, from the circumstance that while there I gathered the fruit of an apple orchard which my father grafted with his own hands, in the first year of the siege of Boston, when he removed, with his mother, from Roxbury street to Dorchester, out of the reach of the shot of the besieged. He lived for a year, and upwards, in Mr. Morgan's old dwelling house, which stood over a cellar under the house now called Brier Cottage. He afterwards (say in 1790) erected the mansion house, of which Jonathan Pierce was the builder, on the part of that farm which is now owned by the Hon. Marshall P. Wilder. Upon this, in the beginning of the present century, Seth Adams, Esq., a former tenant of mine, introduced the first merino sheep imported into Massachusetts.

Upon the Morgan farm, after it came into my possession, I built three houses. The first, over fifty years ago, was situated on the corner next southerly of Mr. Wilder's, on Washington street. The house, and the garden which I laid out with it, was for the occupation of that elegant gentleman, and early friend of mine, John Ward Gurley, who lived in it, as a tenant, until he received the first appointment of District Attorney of the United States, for Louisiana, when he removed to New Orleans. This has been altered into a more conspicuous place, by Charles Hood, Esq., who now owns it.

In 1813, I built the cottage upon the rock, for my own residence, which is now occupied by Capt. Cobb, the exemplary artillerist. About the same time, I pulled down Morgan's dilapidated house, and put up a farm-house on the cellar. In 1827, as an appendage to my cottage, I erected a stone stable, with a cellar and sturcorary under it. This was built with the conglomerate rocks dug from beneath it, and from its permanence will, I think, last till Sebastopol is taken, and will stand as severe a bombardment.

21

I must now call your attention to another successful experiment, of a different kind. Having had the misfortune to be thrown from a chaise and break my jaw, while confined to my home with my bandaged head, desirous of having a water view if I could, I employed myself in digging a canal through the meadows, the water of which came from under the rock on which my cottage was erected. This was a living spring, always having, even in the driest time, six inches of water in it, and at such times furnishing only a supply that would run through a hole as big as a pipe-stem. The constant supply from this source was aided by temporary accessions from a dry brook, or rather from a brook which run only in wet times. The length and dimensions of this canal I afterwards enlarged, and found the water sufficient, except in the very driest periods. It is somewhat remarkable that this little spring is one of the sources of Stony Brook, in West Roxbury, which runs in a serpentine course through a piece of meadow, which I purchased for the purpose. The enlargement of this brook, though at a distance, gives me a delightful water view from the windows of my house, on Jamaica Plain, where I now reside.

The success of my experiment in Dorchester, induced me to make a second, which has been just described, and which is more successful than the first.

These two experiments have convinced me, that if the brooks and creeks in the vicinity of Boston were improved in like manner, the beauty of the scenery in our neighborhood would be immeasurably enlarged, and at a trifling cost, too, for the mud from the meadows would pay for the ditching.

The manner in which I became the owner of the Morgan farm (and other lands in Dorchester), a part of which is now IMPROVED, in the largest sense of that term, by Hon. Marshall P. Wilder, is too interesting to be omitted. It was given to me on the death-bed of the late Gov. Sumner, my father, the deed of which, from the time and manner in which it was done, as well as the value of the gift, will ever be as a jewel to me. When he was first taken with a disease of the heart, called angina pectoris, he was impressed with the conviction that it would prove fatal. He called me to his bed-side, and said to me he did not intend to make a Will, and that it was his wish that I should have a larger portion of his estates than my sisters, and told me to write a Deed, to myself, of the Dorchester farm. I was so overcome by the evidence this afforded of his own conviction he would not recover, that I could not hold a pen or indite a sentence. Seeing my perturbation, he asked me to give him a blank deed and a book to write upon. I could not find a blank, and he, saying there was no time to be lost, sat up in his bed, and with perfect composure wrote out the Deed, on the 16th March, 1799, of the three pieces of land, before named—also, the Merrifield farm, of about sixty acres, at the upper part of the town, on the banks of the Neponset, and the pew in the Meeting-house, all the estate he owned in Dorchester—to his only son, who fears he shall not be able to be present to unite with his father's old friends and neighbors, who, with himself, he hopes, will never cease to bless his memory. The pew which my father gave me was in the Meeting-house of the Parish formerly Mr. Maverick's. This parish gave birth to your distinguished orator, and there I have often heard his uncle, who was its Pastor, preach. My pew was in the building which preceded the highly ornamented Meeting-house, founded on a rock hard by, and if compared with the thatched Meeting-house of the Rev. Mr. Maverick, used for a powder magazine, would lead him to doubt, if he could behold it, whether he was in his own parish. I propose to you, for a toast :—

*The First Parish in Dorchester*—Should there be any attempt in future to blow up its union, may its result, as in the Rev. Mr. Maverick's time, be a MERE FLASH IN THE PAN.

I am respectfully,

Your obedient serv't,

WM. H. SUMNER.

---

Letters were received from the following gentlemen, declining the invitation on account of previous engagements — and enclosing the sentiments annexed.

From John T. Heard, Esq., Boston —

*The United States of America.* — Fanatics and demagogues will labor in vain for their disunion, while the people hold in veneration the memory and teachings of Washington.

From Ex-Governor Hubbard, of New Hampshire —

*The Orator of the Day* — A faithful, untiring and intelligent Watchman on the walls of American Freedom.

From Hon. Isaac Toucey, of Connecticut —

*The Constitution of the United States* — The crowning glory of American Independence. Without abating one jot or tittle from it, we will defend it to the last extremity.

Similar letters were received from the following named gentlemen :—

Hon. Samuel H. Walley,
" J. Wiley Edmands,
Hon. Wm. L. Marcy, Sec'y of State,
Jefferson Davis, Secretary of War,
R. McClelland, Sec'y of the Interior,
Hon. George M. Dallas,
" Theron Metcalf,
" Peleg Sprague,
" Lemuel Shaw,
Franklin Haven, Esq.,
Hon. C. H. Peaslee, Coll. of Boston,
Rev. Jared Sparks, LL.D.,
T. W. Harris, M.D., Cambridge,
Hon. J. H. Clifford, Att. Gen., Mass.,
Hon. B. F. Thomas, Worcester,
" Levi Lincoln, do.
Jacob Foss, Esq., Charlestown,
Hon. Geo. H. Kuhn, Boston,
" James Savage,
" Henry Wilson,
Rev. Mark Hopkins, D.D., Pres. Williams College,
Hon. Thos. Bragg, of N. C.,
Wm. H. Prescott, LL.D.,
Hon. Pliny Merrick,
Washington Irving, Esq.,
Mayors of Lowell, Salem, Lynn, Cambridge, Roxbury,

His Excellency, M. H. Clark, Gov. of New York,
His Excellency Gov. Pollock, Pa.,
" " Gov. Minor, of Conn.,
Hon. Abbott Lawrence,
Professor Joseph Henry, Sec'y Smithsonian Institute, Washington,
Professor A. D. Bache, do.,
Edwin Croswell, Esq., N. Y.,
Hon. H. N. Byington,
" Gorham Brooks, Medford,
Hon. John Whipple, Rhode Island,
Rev. George Putnam, D.D.,
Peter C. Brooks, Esq.,
A number of the officers of the U. S. Army and Navy, stationed in and near Boston,
J. C. Warren, M.D., Boston,
Several Members of Congress,
Hon. Isaac Adams,
Seth Adams, Esq.,
Rev. S. K. Lothrop, D.D.

---

In conformity with the votes passed at the close of the festivities, as mentioned on page 132, letters were written by the Secretary of the Executive Committee, Nahum Capen, Esq., to the Chairman of the Dorchester School Committee, to the Chief Engineer of the Dorchester Fire Department, to the Commanders of the Independent Cadets and the Boston Light Artillery, to the Chief Marshal of the Day, and also to the Chairman of the Committee on Music, conveying copies of the votes, and also expressive of the general appreciation of the acceptable manner in which their several duties were performed. The hope was likewise expressed that this seventy-ninth anniversary of the "*great and good day*" in Dorchester, might contribute to the "honor and freedom of the Republic and the permanency of the Union."

At a meeting of the Executive Committee, July 19th, 1855, a vote of thanks was passed to Col. Enoch Train "for the lively interest which he has manifested in the late celebration; especially for his liberality in erecting on Meeting-house Hill a magnificent flag-staff, from the top of which floated on that occasion a splendid national banner." It was also suggested that this token of Col. Train's munificence "be placed in the keeping of the town, to be used on the return of our national birth-day and other proper occasions." It was likewise resolved that "a metallic band, with a suitable inscription, be affixed to the flag-staff, as a testimonial of the regard of this Committee for the patriotism and liberality of its worthy donor."

---

The festivities and rejoicings of a day long to be remembered by the citizens of Dorchester, were closed by a magnificent display of Fireworks in the evening, on Mt. Bowdoin, under the general management of the committee appointed for the purpose, and by a Levee at the house of Gov. Gardner.

---

### CORRECTIONS.

It is stated, page 46, that Israel Stoughton "built the first tide-mill for grinding corn in the Colony." The word "tide" should be omitted. The mill was at the lower falls of the Neponset.

In the list of Officers and Committees, page 89, the name of Alpheus Hardy, Esq., should have been inserted among the Vice-Presidents.

www.ingramcontent.com/pod-product-compliance
Lightning Source LLC
LaVergne TN
LVHW021400110826
845150LV00007B/1734

* 9 7 8 1 4 2 5 5 1 3 1 6 0 *